SO-BNB-409

To my one and only, happy twentieth anniversary, love.

Twenty-First Century Books
A division of Lerner Publishing Group, Inc.
241 First Avenue North
Minneapolis, MN 55401 USA

For reading levels and more information, look up this title at www.lernerbooks.com.

Main body text set in Adobe Garamond Pro 11.5/15
Typeface provided by Adobe Systems.

Library of Congress Cataloging-in-Publication Data

Names: Keyser, Amber, author.
Title: Tying the knot : a world history of marriage / by Amber J. Keyser.
Description: Minneapolis : Twenty-First Century Books, [2017] | Includes
    bibliographical references and index: LCCN 2016019334 (print) | LCCN
    2016029916 (ebook) | ISBN 9781467792424 (lb : alk. paper) | ISBN 9781512428469
    (eb pdf)
Subjects: LCSH: Marriage—History—Juvenile literature. | Marriage customs and
    rites—Juvenile literature.
Classification: LCC HQ744 .K46 2017 (print) | LCC HQ744 (ebook) | DDC
    306.810973—dc23

LC record available at https://lccn.loc.gov/2016019334

Manufactured in the United States of America
1-38270-19999-6/12/2017

CONTENTS

Introduction
CONTROL FREAKS

In 2011 Prince William, the Duke of Cambridge and second in line to inherit the throne of the United Kingdom (also called Britain), married Catherine (Kate) Middleton in London's Westminster Abbey. Thousands attended the elaborate ceremony. Nearly one billion people watched it live on television and on YouTube. Members of the wedding party traveled in horse-drawn carriages, cheered on by crowds of well-wishers. The bride's lacy white dress had a long train, and her delicate veil was held in place with a sparkling tiara. The groom wore the scarlet uniform of the Irish Guards, one of the military units he belongs to, and a cap with the motto of the regiment: Quis Separabit? which means "Who shall separate us?"

At the altar, William and Kate held hands and exchanged rings, and the Archbishop of Canterbury united them in marriage. Kate became a princess and, as the wife of the royal heir, the likely future queen. The world reveled in the lavish spectacle of this royal love story. It was a fairy tale come to life.

The world celebrated along with Britain's Prince William and Catherine Middleton when they married in 2011.

FORGET THE FAIRY TALE

Love and marriage are all around us. Pop singers croon about romance. Magazines offer advice on finding love and making it last. News outlets and websites track the latest gossip on celebrity marriages (and divorces). Millions of viewers tune in to *The Bachelor,* a TV show that is supposed to end with a marriage proposal. Marriage is one of the oldest institutions on the planet. It is the basis for family life in nearly every human society. And marriage is all about love, right?

Wrong!

For centuries, getting married wasn't a private decision between two people. Families, neighbors, religious leaders, warlords, and other rulers all had their fingers in the pie. The government in France in the mid-sixteenth century, for example, declared that marriage was "a public act transmitting family property, sanctioned [approved] by the state, and tied to the public good." That doesn't sound very romantic, does it?

By all accounts, Prince William and his wife are genuinely in love, but because he is in line to become king, his decision to marry her wasn't entirely his own. According to the Royal Marriages Act of 1772, Prince William had to obtain permission to marry from the ruling monarch, Queen Elizabeth II, his grandmother. The original goal of the Royal Marriages Act was to ensure that all royal marriages benefited Britain politically or economically.

THE BUILDING BLOCK OF SOCIETY

Marriage is the legally recognized union of two people as a single unit. This unit is the core building block of almost every society on the planet. Throughout history and across cultures, political, economic, and social systems have all been cemented through marriage.

Politically, royal marriages in Britain and elsewhere were meant to seal alliances between different families, tribes, kingdoms, or countries. For example, a monarch might send a princess to marry a neighboring ruler to strengthen the relationship between the two kingdoms. A conquering warlord might marry the daughter of a ruler he had just overthrown to confirm his victory.

Economically, families used marriage to protect their money and property. Typically, a son (sometimes only the eldest son) inherited his father's wealth, thus ensuring that all the assets accumulated by the men of the family stayed within the family. Any women who married into a wealthy family were expected to produce male children to guarantee the survival of the male line and therefore the protection of the family's wealth.

Socially, marriage gave a green light to sexual relations and provided a family structure for raising children. A child conceived within the confines of marriage was viewed as "legitimate," or legal. According to both religious and civil (nonreligious) law, that child was an official member of the family. A child conceived outside of marriage—in an adulterous or premarital relationship—

*This photograph from 1869 shows a Chinese bride (*right*) in her wedding clothes, accompanied by a servant. Throughout the centuries, marriage has cemented social, political, and economic bonds.*

was viewed as "illegitimate" and was not legally part of the family. An illegitimate son of a king could not ascend to the throne on the death of his father. An illegitimate son could not inherit his father's wealth.

In most cultures in earlier eras, women had no legal rights and could not own property. Their financial security and social status came first from their fathers and then—after marriage—from their husbands. Young women who didn't marry were often pushed to the edges of society. Neighbors viewed them with suspicion and scorn. Some unmarried women lived with their elderly parents. Others joined religious orders. Still others became prostitutes.

WHAT'S LOVE GOT TO DO WITH IT?

Throughout most of human history, love and marriage rarely went together. Men chose brides who could advance their political, economic, and social standing. Usually women did not choose their husbands at all. Fathers arranged their marriages. For thousands of years and across many cultures, daughters were considered the property of their fathers. Marriage was an act that legally transferred property (a daughter) from father to husband. Whether a woman loved or even liked the man her father had picked didn't matter. If her father demanded it, a daughter was powerless to refuse the union. Around the world, many modern marriage traditions reflect this history of property transaction. In many nations, a man asks the father of his beloved for permission to marry her. In the United States and elsewhere, we talk about the father "giving away the bride" at a wedding ceremony.

Earlier societies—and still many modern ones—were strictly divided by class, race, and religion. To maintain these divisions, institutions of church and state forbade certain marriages. Catholics could not wed non-Catholics. Blacks could not marry whites. Had Prince William and Catherine Middleton lived when the Royal Marriages Act was passed, the ruling British monarch would likely have forbidden their union. Kate is a commoner—her family does not belong to the British nobility. In earlier eras, a prince's marriage to a commoner would have offered Britain no political alliances or economic benefits.

But marriage has changed over the centuries, and the biggest change involves love. When it comes to finding a marriage partner, twenty-first-century couples want to feel butterflies in their stomachs. They want soul mates and romance. That's not to say that all marriages of the past were loveless life sentences. If a couple was lucky, love and marriage coincided. The difference between history and modern times is that in the past, being in love wasn't a reason to get married.

The addition of love to the marriage contract began about 250 years ago. Around then, especially in Europe and North America, society was changing. Commoners began to push against monarchies in favor of democratically elected governments. They

WALKING MARRIAGE

For the Mosuo people of Yunnan Province in southwestern China, siblings—not married couples—form the foundation of a family. Brothers and sisters live together with their mother and their maternal aunts and uncles (their mother's brothers and sisters), even as adults, and even after they have married their spouses. The spouses live in different homes with their own brothers, sisters, mothers, and maternal aunts and uncles. When a married couple has children, the children are considered members of the mother's household.

Thirty-four-year-old Nazhu Zhuoma and her husband, Zhaba Songding, have a typical Mosuo marriage. They live in a village called Luoshui, and their relationship, like all marital unions in their village, is called a walking marriage. Every evening Zhaba walks from his mother's house, where he lives with his siblings, to his wife's house, where he spends the night. In the morning, he reverses the trip to spend the day at his mother's house.

In Mosuo families, women make most of the big decisions, such as what to do with a family business or whether to have a child. For instance, Nazhu runs a lakeside hotel and manages her family's finances. Zhaba is an involved father to their two children, but he has no legal claim to them. They take their last name from their mother. Nor is Nazhu bound to be faithful to her husband. Mosuo women may choose to have more than one sexual partner. Since family lineage is traced through the maternal line, no one keeps track of who fathered which children.

didn't want kings, nobles, and church leaders making all the decisions about politics and family life. With the rise of democratic governments, old rules about marriage began falling away. And women began to push for equal rights with men. Although it took several centuries for women to win those rights, the movement for women's equality brought many changes to the institution of marriage. Couples began to marry for love, and women had more freedom to choose their own partners.

Modern weddings can be simple or elaborate, low cost or wildly expensive. Some couples spend more than $500 on the cake alone.

The fairy-tale wedding of Prince William and Catherine Middleton in 2011 was a bridge between the institution of marriage as it had existed for most of human history and the quirky, evolving institution we know in the West in the twenty-first century. For the fascinating details that got us from then to now, set aside the tuxedo, the diamond ring, and the cake smooshing and take a walk down the aisle into the unexpected history of marriage.

1
WHY PLAY THE GAME?

In 2015 archaeologists from Mississippi State University, excavating near Alepotrypa Cave in Greece, discovered two ancient skeletons locked in an embrace. Genetic testing revealed that one was a man and the other a woman. In the excavated grave, the male skeleton rested behind the female with his arms around her, in the spooning position that sweethearts often assume when cuddling. Archaeologists dated the skeletons to about 3800 BCE.

Had the man and woman loved each other when they were alive? Had they had children together? Had they been joined in something resembling a marriage before being buried together in death? Archaeologists can only guess at the answers. The society to which this couple belonged left no written records, but their embrace in death suggests that they also had a lasting bond in life. We know more about relationships that occurred after humans started writing things down, which first happened around 3300 BCE in the ancient Middle East. By this time, marriage was a common institution. How did it get started and why?

WORKING SIDE BY SIDE

When trying to piece together the origins of marriage, anthropologists (scientists who study human societies) examine ideas about the lifestyles of our distant ancestors. Before the development of agriculture in the Middle East about ten thousand years ago, most humans were hunter-gatherers. They traveled from place to place, following herds of game animals and gathering wild roots, nuts, berries, and other plant parts for food. Extended family members lived in small bands, numbering from a few to perhaps one hundred individuals.

But what about marriage?

In the twentieth century, some anthropologists proposed that marriage originated because women in preagricultural societies were physically weak. According to this idea, women needed men to hunt game for meat and to protect them and their children from wild animals and other dangers. In return, women offered sex and offspring to men. Marriages cemented this exchange. Other

The San people of southern Africa still live much like their ancestors did, by hunting and gathering. Anthropologists think that marriages likely fostered cooperation among different hunter-gatherer bands.

researchers suggested a different explanation. They said that women in ancient hunter-gatherer societies had valuable skills that men needed, such as knowledge about which plants were safe to eat. To corner this resource, men captured women or coerced them into marriage.

Both these explanations are based on an assumption about hunter-gatherer societies: that they divided labor along gender lines. In other words, men did dangerous tasks such as hunting mammoths. Women did more peaceful work, such as nursing babies and picking berries. But twenty-first-century researchers say this reasoning is faulty because it is based on modern assumptions about the typical gender roles we assign to men and women.

In most parts of the world, hunting and gathering gave way to agriculture thousands of years ago. Some groups in North America, Africa, Asia, and South America retained a hunter-gather lifestyle well into the nineteenth century, and a few groups still live by hunting and gathering. By studying the artwork, clothing, and traditions of these groups, anthropologists can speculate about life in ancient hunter-gatherer societies. Linda Owen, an anthropologist at the University of Tübingen in Germany, concludes that the roles of women and men probably overlapped in ancient times. Owen believes that both genders likely gathered food and hunted game, especially small animals such as rabbits and birds. In North America, many Plains Indians lived as hunter-gatherers into the mid-nineteenth century. Scholars say that among these groups, everyone in a band—men, women, and children—took part in buffalo hunts. This research suggests that ancient hunter-gatherers needed one another too much to divide jobs by gender.

Another theory about ancient hunter-gatherers is that unions between two people of different bands linked the two groups together. Anthropologists say that these friendly connections ensured that when bands ran into each other at vital water holes or oyster beds, they shared resources instead of fighting over them.

MANY HANDS MAKE LIGHT THE WORK

Once humans settled down and began to farm the land, social dynamics changed. The intense work of preparing the soil, planting, tending, and harvesting crops, caring for animals, and preserving food to last through the winter required many hands laboring together. A couple could do more than a single person, and having children meant more able bodies to share the work. The talents and assets a potential spouse could bring to the partnership were paramount. A skilled cheese maker could be a worthy wife, and a man with a large plot of land was a valued husband. Marriage took on an added role: building the family workforce.

The rise of agriculture also set the stage for economic inequality. With individual families each working their own land, the fortunes of an entire community no longer rose or fell together. Farming families with access to rich soil and plenty of water for crops harvested the bounty. They stored extra food for lean times. Their children were well fed. They earned money from selling surplus crops. A family whose patch of land was rocky and dry struggled to grow enough to eat. Hard seasons with poor yields meant no extra income and could even mean starvation and death.

The differentiation between haves and have-nots continued as farms, towns, and cities developed around the world. Marriage took on a new job—to help secure wealth within families. Rich families didn't want to drag down their fortunes by linking up with poor families. So the rich married the rich, and the poor married the poor.

CONSOLIDATING POWER

The powerful, who were usually rich, married the powerful. In the eighteenth century BCE, a leader named Zimri-Lim conquered the city of Mari in Mesopotamia (which later became Iraq and parts of Syria and Turkey). He declared himself king, dumped his wife, and married the daughter of a neighboring ruler. He wed each of his eight daughters to the rulers of nearby cities. In agreeing to the matches, the husbands also agreed to hand over their authority to Zimri-Lim. Each man's wedding document stated, "He is the husband of Zimri-Lim's daughter and he obeys Zimri-Lim." The men agreed to the marriages because they feared Zimri-Lim's power.

This tradition of marrying daughters to other rulers continued over the centuries. The opinions of the daughters involved held little or no sway. They were rarely more than pawns in a chess game of political power. In 1514, for example, Princess Isabella of Austria, only thirteen years old, was wed to King Christian II of Denmark (then aged thirty-three) to forge an alliance between their two nations. She traveled to Denmark to marry a man she had never met. Isabella wrote to her sister beforehand, "It is hard enough to marry a man . . . whom you do not know or love, and worse still to be required to leave home and kindred [family], and follow a stranger to the ends of the earth, without even being able to speak his language."

Belgian painter Bernard van Orley made this portrait of Isabella of Austria, who was wed as a teenager in 1514 to King Christian II of Denmark. Her father arranged her marriage to the king to ally the two royal families.

FOLLOW THE MONEY

Most ancient cultures were organized around patriarchal inheritance in which property passed down from father to son (often only to the eldest son). What if a man died without leaving a male heir? What if his widow remarried and transferred her dead husband's land and money to her new husband? Such a scenario worried the Hebrews of the ancient Middle East. As described in the Bible, their solution was to require the widow and her dead husband's brother to get married. This practice, called a levirate marriage, kept money and land in the same family.

Property and money weren't the only things passed down from father to son. Beginning in the Middle Ages in Europe (around 400 to 1500 CE), noblemen, such as dukes and earls—positions that held political power—passed on their privileged status to the eldest son after death. If the nobleman was a king or emperor, his eldest son (or sometimes the eldest daughter if the ruler left no male heirs) became the ruler after his death. Unlike in a democratic government, common people had no say in the

LEVIRATE MARRIAGES

In some places, the tradition of levirate marriages has continued into modern times. From the woman's perspective, a levirate marriage is often repressive and difficult. Ram Chander, who lives in the Karnal District of northern India, described the levirate marriage of his grandmother in the twentieth century. She was widowed at eighteen, and custom dictated that she marry her dead husband's brother, who was only three years old. She raised this child, who was also her husband, and at some point had children with him. The tradition of levirate marriage, which persists in a few cultures in the twenty-first century, perpetuates the view of women as property that can be transferred from man to man within a family.

transfer of power. For those born into a noble or ruling family, it was critically important to protect their power. They married their children to the children of other powerful and wealthy people. This ensured that power and wealth were passed on to the next generations.

When taken to the extreme, intermarriage for the sake of keeping money and power in the same family sometimes had serious medical consequences. People in the same family carry many of the same genes (structures inside cells that determine a person's physical traits and that are passed on from parent to child). If two cousins marry and both carry a gene for a particular disease, their children might develop that disease.

From 1516 to 1700, the Hapsburg family ruled Spain. To keep power within the family, cousins often married cousins and uncles often married nieces. Medical historians think that marriages between members of the Hapsburg family led to genetic disorders that passed from one generation to the next. The last in the family line of Hapsburg rulers was Charles II (1661–1700). Historians believe that he inherited disorders that harmed his mental and physical health. He didn't learn to talk until he was four years old and didn't walk until he was eight. He didn't grow properly, was often sick, and was apparently infertile (unable to conceive children). For these reasons, the Spanish people called him El Hechizado—the Hexed.

BE FRUITFUL AND MULTIPLY

According to the Bible, Adam and Eve, the official First Couple of the Jewish, Christian, and Islamic traditions, had a very important job. God ordered them to populate the newly created Earth with their children. In Genesis, the first book of the Bible, God promises Abraham that his descendants will be as numerous as the stars in the sky.

OLD-STYLE MATCH.COM

Between 1763 and 1944, European nobles looking for a marriage partner could consult a reference book called the *Almanach de Gotha* (*below*). Originated by a German chaplain in the city of Gotha, the book sorted and ranked all members of European noble families in great detail. Families used the book to determine which matches were acceptable. Specifically, marriage partners were supposed to be of the same rank—that is, a duke was supposed to marry the daughter of a duke, not the daughter of a man of lower rank. If a man did choose a lower-ranked wife, he entered into what was called a left-hand marriage. During the wedding ceremony, he held the bride's right hand with his left hand instead of the traditional right hand.

In 1998 a British company issued a new edition of the *Almanach de Gotha*, but critics noted that it was sloppily written. And even though some Europeans still inherit titles of nobility, these titles are mostly symbolic. For instance, the United Kingdom still has a queen, princes, dukes, earls, and other nobles, but they no longer run the country. Instead, citizens of the United Kingdom vote for their leaders. Since it's no longer necessary to maintain power by marrying into another royal family, European nobles no longer have reason to consult the *Almanach de Gotha*.

ALMANACH
DE
GOTHA.

ANNUAIRE
DIPLOMATIQUE ET STATISTIQUE
POUR L'ANNÉE
1869.

CENT-SIXIÈME ANNÉE.

Pour la vente en dehors du duché de Gotha.

Judaism, Christianity, and Islam all view the production of children as an integral part of marriage. For most of human history, it was also an inevitable part of the union. Before the 1960s, when women first had legal access to birth control, the only sure way for a woman to avoid pregnancy was to avoid sex. But wives were considered the property of their husbands, so refusing sex was not usually an option. Women of the past were often pregnant or nursing babies for the majority of their adult lives. Childbirth was often perilous for both mother and baby. Childbirth was the leading cause of death for women for most of human history and still is in certain parts of the world. Without birth control, women had no choice but to accept the risks.

In ancient Greece, the wife's job as a bearer of babies was declared from the start. During wedding ceremonies, the father of the bride announced, "I give you this woman for the procreation of legitimate children." The groom responded, "I take her." After her wedding, an upper-class Greek wife lived in a women-only part of the house, from which she hardly ever emerged. Her husband visited her for sex, in the hopes of conceiving male heirs. At the same time, Greek husbands kept mistresses called hetaerae, who accompanied them in public.

Infertility was a cause of great shame. In many cultures, if a wife failed to produce children, her husband was entitled to divorce her. Empress Josephine of France (1763–1814) is a good example. Even though she and her husband, Emperor Napoleon Bonaparte, loved each other, he divorced her in 1810 because she had failed to provide him with a male heir—or any children at all.

This stone marks the grave of a wealthy woman from ancient Greece. She is shown (seated) with a female servant. As an upper-class woman, her married life was likely very limited. She would have been confined to the house most of the time. Her primary job was to bear children.

The stigma of infertility was so great in earlier eras that some societies viewed childless women as witches or as possessed by demons. And the stigma and shame didn't apply only to women. Male impotence—the inability to have sexual intercourse—was also seen as a failure, serious enough to be grounds for divorce. The Catholic Church, which dictated much about family life in Europe for many centuries, recommended the following procedure to confirm impotence: "The man and woman are to be placed together in one bed and wise women are to be summoned around the bed for many nights. And if the man's member [penis] is always found useless and as if dead, the couple are well able to be separated."

"STRANGLIEST INCHANTED"

The ancient Greeks thought that romantic love was a form of madness. So did the French during the Middle Ages. In ancient India, romantic passion was seen as downright antisocial. Anyone who has been in love knows that it's wild and unpredictable, intoxicating and thrilling. But being swept off your feet or blinded by love can leave a person feeling unstable and out of control. Because of these feelings, many early cultures viewed passionate love as a threat to the real goals of marriage—building political alliances, protecting family wealth, and having children.

The ideal marriage in earlier eras was one that fostered the growth of a companionable, friendly warmth between well-matched partners *after* they had tied the knot. When married couples actually appeared to be passionate about each other, family and friends were often dismayed. In the seventeenth century in the North American colony of Virginia, for example, one man noted that a woman he observed "was more fond of her husband perhaps than the Politeness of the day allows." Another young man was appalled to see that his uncle was "the strangliest inchanted [most strangely enchanted] and infatuated in his first marriage that I think ever any wise man was."

DOUBLE STANDARDS

In historic eras (and continuing into the twenty-first century in some cultures), sex before marriage was seen as a sin—especially for women. A woman or girl who had premarital sex might be punished, shunned, or even put to death. If she got pregnant, she was disgraced. Her children were called bastards and had no rights to their father's family name or inheritance. Illegitimate births in some ancient cultures were considered so shameful that women often abandoned or even murdered their babies. The men who impregnated these women were rarely subject to shame or punishment, however. The prohibition against sex before marriage is an example of a double standard—a rule that is enforced with one group and not another.

Adultery—or sex with someone other than one's spouse—is forbidden by the Ten Commandments, rules for living that, according to biblical accounts, was given to Moses by God in the ancient Middle East. Like rules about premarital sex, the commandments were also a double standard. In the ancient Middle East, for example, the commandment against adultery meant one thing for wives and another for husbands. For the woman, adultery meant having sex with anyone other than her husband. The man was guilty only if he slept with another man's wife. Then he was thought to have violated that man's property rights. The punishment for adultery in biblical times was usually death by stoning or fire. The ancient Romans also had different sexual standards for women and men. A man was free to cheat sexually on his spouse. But according to Roman law, if a man found his wife in bed with someone else, he could do whatever he wanted: kill her, beat her, divorce her, or forgive her.

> The prohibition against sex before marriage is an example of a double standard—a rule that is enforced with one group and not another.

The sexual double standard remains in place in the twenty-first century. In some nations, women are still shunned and punished for having sex outside of marriage. In the United States, girls and women aren't usually punished for having sex, but they are applauded for remaining virgins until marriage. In a ritual known as a purity ball, some American girls pledge to abstain from sex until marriage and their fathers commit to protecting their virginity. Friends and family praise and respect the virgins. Meanwhile, girls who do have sex before marriage—especially if they have multiple partners—might be called sluts. But few people condemn a boy or man who has many sexual partners. They might even admire him for being a "ladies' man."

Even so, history and literature are full of love stories like that of the legendary characters of Odysseus and Penelope in Greek myth. They were so devoted to each other that he refused the love of a goddess. She denied one hundred eager suitors. More often, though, marriage came first and loving companionship followed after—if a couple was lucky. This sequence of events—marriage before love—made many marriages more stable. Instead of focusing on romance, couples put their energy into children, work, and the extended family. If the relationship was practical, friendly, and even businesslike, couples were usually in it for the long haul.

A PRIVATE RELATIONSHIP

The revolutionary idea of a love-based union began to take hold in the eighteenth century. Part of this shift was related to political movements and revolutions. In the West (Europe and North America), democratic ideals were on the rise. Kings were falling out of favor—and out of power—often through war. During the American Revolution (1775–1783), for example, North American colonists wrested power from the British monarch and set up a government in which white men voted for their political leaders. This democratic trend had been taking hold in the home as well. Women were less and less satisfied that a man was the sole ruler of the family. In 1706 British writer Mary Astell asked, "If Absolute Sovereignty [all authority vested in one ruler] be not necessary in a State, how comes it to be so in a Family?" The world was a long way from equality between men and women, but the conversation had begun.

Another force shaking up traditional ideas about marriage was the Romantic movement. It started in Europe at the end of the eighteenth century. This school of thought was a reaction against an increasingly mechanized, science-oriented, and commercialized world. Instead of viewing marriage as an economic and political decision, individuals began to see marriage as a private, romantic relationship based on feelings and emotion. The new measure of a marriage's success was not business deals or treaties but happiness. Couples wanted to make their own decisions, and they were looking for romance and passion. Picking a spouse based on love became the ideal rather than a threat to social order. A woman's feelings toward her husband mattered, and at least in the West, forced marriage was on the way out.

The movement for women's rights also accompanied the gradual shift from marriages based on economics to marriages based on love. The first US women's rights convention, organized by Lucretia Mott and Elizabeth Cady Stanton, took place in Seneca Falls, New York, in 1848. US women won the right to vote in 1920, with the ratification of the Nineteenth Amendment to the US Constitution. During World War II (1939–1945), US women joined the workforce in large numbers, taking factory jobs that had previously been

This colorized photograph shows women demonstrating for the right to vote in New York City in 1912. US women won that right in 1920. As American women gained more political rights, they gained more authority in their marriages as well.

held by men. In 1960 the US Food and Drug Administration approved the newly developed birth control pill, freeing women from unwanted pregnancies. But many laws still restricted women's rights, kept women from entering certain professions, and limited their options in schooling, sports, and political activities. During the women's liberation movement of the 1960s and 1970s, women successfully fought to have these laws changed. Earlier in the century, a woman usually had to get married to attain financial security and social approval. Love didn't always figure into that equation. But with the women's movement opening up new social, professional, and financial opportunities, women could choose marriage on their own terms.

TILL DEATH DO US PART

The changes in the institution of marriage over the last two hundred years have been seismic. Perhaps one of the most startling is the increasing number of people, especially in the United States of the twenty-first century, who choose not to get married at all. According to US census data, in 1967, more than 70 percent of adults lived with a spouse. In 2015 the number was barely over 50 percent. The percentage of unmarried adults living together as a couple showed an opposite trend, rising from barely 1 percent to nearly 10 percent during the same time period.

In the twenty-first century, the old reasons for marriage, such as inheritance, alliance building, economic necessity, and child rearing, are less important. In most of the West, women can support themselves without a husband. As the number of divorces has risen, single-parent homes have become more common. Children born out of wedlock are rarely called illegitimate anymore, and they have the same legal rights as any other children. And except for the Duke and Duchess of Cambridge (William and Kate), few people worry about passing on noble rank to the next generation.

So why do people still get married?

Partly it's because we like the new-and-improved story of falling in love and living happily ever after. Also, at least in the United States, society and government favor married people over single individuals. The US General Accounting Office lists more than one thousand federal laws that grant benefits to married couples. For example, married couples can pass property to each other without paying taxes on the exchange. In some states, a married person can assign lottery winnings to a spouse without paying gift taxes. The legal spouse of a person who is sick or injured can get critical information from doctors and make key medical decisions without special permission, but for an unmarried partner written permission is needed.

The upshot is that when a couple in the United States faces big decisions or life-or-death situations, a marriage license is a safety net. It helps the couple protect and care for each other. It also says that a community approves of that couple's love for each other. That can make marriage very appealing.

2
MORE WAYS THAN ONE

In April 2012, Jacob Zuma, the seventy-year-old president of South Africa, returned to his home village in the province of KwaZulu-Natal to celebrate his marriage to businesswoman Gloria Ngema. Zuma is a member of the Zulu ethnic group, and he married Ngema in a traditional Zulu ceremony called *umgcagco*. He wore a leopard-skin cloak and carried a leaf-shaped shield. She wore bright colors—red, yellow, and green. They celebrated their union with drums and traditional dancing in front of a crowd of smiling friends and relatives. At the wedding reception that evening, having changed into Western-style clothes, the couple cut a three-tiered, white-frosted cake and the dancing continued. The following day was the *umabo*, a Zulu custom during which the bride gives gifts to the groom's family.

Throughout the celebrations, the couple was joined by Jacob Zuma's three other wives. (The president has been married six times. He is divorced from one wife, and another is dead.) South Africa is the only country in the world to have four official first ladies.

South African president Jacob Zuma with his three wives in 2009. The women (from left to right) are Nompumelo Ntuli, Thobeka Mabhija, and Sizakele Khumalo. Zuma married a fourth wife, Gloria Ngema, in 2012.

THE MORE THE MERRIER?

Western norms of marriage are focused on monogamy, or being married to only one person at a time. (*Mono* comes from a Greek word meaning "single," or "one.") This is the typical form of marriage in the United States, the countries of Europe, and other Western, industrialized nations in the twenty-first century. Monogamous heterosexual couples consist of one woman and one man. Same-sex marriages—monogamous unions between two people of the same gender—are increasingly common. But monogamy was not always the norm.

Polygamy (*gamy* comes from a Greek word meaning "to marry") and *plural marriage* are general terms for marriages of more than two people. When one man marries multiple women, like Jacob Zuma, the practice is called polygyny. (In Greek, *poly* means "many" and *gyny* refers to "women.") For thousands of years and in many different places, humans commonly entered into polygynous marriages. By marrying multiple women, a man enjoyed multiple sexual relationships; had more family members to help run his farm, business, or household; and ideally fathered more sons who would inherit his name, status, and wealth.

The history of polygyny begins with Abraham, whose story is told in the biblical book of Genesis. According to the Bible, he was married to three women—Sarah, Hagar, and Keturah. The Bible also describes many other cases of polygynous marriage, which was common among the ancient Hebrews.

The Hindu religion developed in India around 1500 BCE. The early Hindus also practiced polygyny. But because it was expensive to maintain multiple wives and children, only wealthy men could afford to do so.

Buddhism, a major religion founded around 400 BCE in India, has never prohibited or promoted any form of marriage. Instead, cultural traditions of specific regions where Buddhism was practiced dictated marriage customs. In ancient China, for instance, Buddhist rulers and noblemen often had one official wife and many mistresses with whom they fathered children.

Since its inception in the first century CE, the Christian Church has promoted monogamous unions. Based on the biblical story of Adam and Eve, early church leaders promoted a one-man-with-one-woman model of marriage.

The Islamic religion was founded by the prophet Muhammad in Arabia in the seventh century CE. He had multiple wives, and the Quran, the Muslim holy book of Islam, says that a man should take no more than four wives at a time. Muslim men were not required or urged to take more than one wife, but the practice was allowed as long as all wives were treated with equal love and attention. Scholars note that warfare sometimes left many Muslim women without husbands or fathers to care for them. These women were better off socially and economically if they married, even if the man already had other wives.

ONE ON ONE

Over time, marriage practices began to change. Jews abandoned polygyny around 1000 CE when Rabbi Gershom ben Judah, a Jewish teacher and spiritual leader in what became Germany, established a series of guidelines for Jewish family life. His rules included a prohibition against polygyny. According to religious scholars, the ban was intended to strengthen the family unit. Whereas a man with multiple wives and many children might not have enough money to support them, a man with just one wife could devote more resources to his family. And, scholars say, the ban discouraged a man from neglecting or abusing one wife thinking that he could simply marry another one if he was unhappy.

Over time, as Christianity spread, Christians continued to practice monogamy, with one exception. The Church of Jesus Christ of Latter-day Saints, also called the LDS Church, or the Mormons, is a Christian sect founded by Joseph Smith in New York in 1830. Smith believed that God had communicated with him directly. God's rules for living, according to Smith, included

ALL FOR ALL

Group marriage, in which multiple men marry multiple women, is a relatively rare form of plural marriage. From 1848 to 1879, members of the Oneida Community, a religious society in New York State, practiced an extreme form of group marriage that they called complex marriage. In this system, every man in the community was married to every woman in the community.

The founder of the community, John Humphrey Noyes, oversaw all the sexual relationships. He assigned the male and female sexual partners and had them change regularly. Not surprisingly, community members disliked some sexual partners and grew attached to others. Jealousy and possessiveness in part led to the community's demise.

More Ways Than One

the practice of polygyny. The LDS Church established several communities in the midwestern United States but clashed with non-Mormons there. Its members eventually left the Midwest and settled in Utah in 1847. Claiming that polygyny was immoral, the US government passed laws against it in the late nineteenth century. The Morrill Anti-Bigamy Act of 1862 banned polygyny in US territories. The Edmunds Anti-Polygamy Act of 1882 made polygyny a crime. At first, the LDS Church resisted the assault on its traditions, but pressure to comply with US law became too great. In 1890 the LDS Church itself renounced polygyny in a document called the Manifesto. Members no longer practice polygyny, although it continues among some groups that have broken from the religion.

A polygynous LDS family of the 1870s. The clan included a man, his two wives, and their nine children. Members of LDS no longer practice polygyny.

To protect women from abusive husbands and to promote equality between spouses, more nations began to outlaw polygamy. Japan did so in 1880, as did mainland China in 1950. Hong Kong, a semiautonomous region of China, made polygamy illegal in 1971. In India the Hindu Marriage Act of 1955 banned polygyny for Hindus. (About 13 percent of India's citizens are Muslims, and the law does not apply to them.)

Still, polygyny continued around the world. During the 1960s, American anthropologist George Murdock surveyed marriage practices in 1,231 different groups around the world. He found that more than one thousand societies—almost 85 percent of those he studied—were polygynous.

But the trend toward monogamy has also continued. In the twenty-first century, most Muslim marriages are monogamous, even though Islamic law permits a man to have more than one wife. Christianity dominates in the West, so monogamy is the only legal form of marriage there. The majority of the countries where polygyny is still legal are in Africa, the Middle East, and Southeast Asia. Even there, polygamous unions occur with less frequency.

In countries where polygyny is illegal, such as the United States, Canada, and the United Kingdom, some Muslims and members of other religious groups marry multiple wives in secret, but the practice is far from widespread. In Israel, where polygyny is also against the law, a small group of Orthodox (traditional) Jews propose reinstating the practice. They reason that if polygyny was okay in biblical times, it should be acceptable in the twenty-first century. They also see polygyny as a way to increase the worldwide population of Jews, since a man with multiple wives can have far more children than a man with just one wife.

THE POLYANDRY EQUATION

The Lahaul Valley is nestled high in the Himalayas at the northernmost tip of India. During the short growing season there, farmers grow peas and potatoes on terraces cut into the steep mountainsides. They harvest apples and plums from their orchards. They also practice polyandry, the marriage of multiple men to a shared wife. (The suffix *andry* comes from a Greek word meaning "man.") Buddhi Devi is one such wife. In 1954, when she was fourteen, Devi was engaged to a boy and his younger brother. She married both of them. Together they farmed the land and raised five children.

The tradition of polyandry goes back many centuries in the valley. It developed as a form of natural population control. A man's ability to father children is nearly limitless if he has multiple female sexual partners. A woman, regardless of the number of sexual partners, can bear only so many babies in a lifetime. So a system of marriage in which many men share the same wife keeps the birthrate down. This was a priority in the Lahaul Valley, with its harsh winters and scarce resources. Overpopulation there could lead to starvation, so a marriage structure that naturally limited the number of children made sense.

Anthropologists have identified more than fifty groups that still practice polyandry. Examples include the Yanomami of South America and the Maasai of East Africa. Several conditions seem to encourage the development of polyandrous cultures. First, if a society has far more men than women, several men—often brothers—can share the sexual and reproductive benefits of having a wife. Second, some societies have very high male death rates. The men may fight in frequent wars or have dangerous jobs. A woman with multiple husbands in such a society won't be left single if one of the husbands dies. Third, in environments with extreme weather or limited natural resources, such as in the Lahaul Valley, it often makes economic sense to limit childbirth rates through polyandry.

But polyandry is fading. Increasing global connectivity and technological advances have brought economic opportunities, medical care, and other resources to once-remote societies. As traditional lifestyles adapt to twenty-first-century technologies, polyandry is no longer essential for survival. None of Buddhi Devi's children have continued the practice.

In a polyandrous marriage, a woman takes more than one husband. A Tibetan woman poses here with her two husbands.

WOMEN AND CHILDREN FIRST

Why has monogamy replaced polygyny as the dominant form of marriage around the world? A 2012 study by researchers at the University of British Columbia in Canada concluded that modern societies where monogamous marriage is the norm benefit from a reduction in crime, including rape, murder, kidnapping, and assault. The researchers note that in polygynous cultures, only upper-class men can afford to marry more than one woman. This situation leaves poor and lower-class men with a smaller pool of marriageable women to choose from. Single men in those communities are more likely to fight one another for the few available women. And the desire for sex among these unmarried men leads some of them to kidnap and rape women. But in monogamous cultures, the ratio of marriageable men and women is closer to fifty-fifty, so men don't have to pursue illegal avenues to find sexual partners.

The study also found that monogamous marriage benefits women and children. In monogamous families, fathers tend to be more devoted to the family because they can focus their attention on just one wife and on fewer children. And women in industrialized societies that practice monogamy tend to get married and have children later than do women in polygynous groups. They are more likely to finish high school or college and have a career, which translates into more economic and social equality between husband and wife.

LET'S DO IT OUR WAY

For much of the twentieth century, the traditional family—a marriage between one man, who usually worked outside the home, and one woman, who usually stayed at home to raise their children—was the norm in the United States. The 1950 US census revealed that 78 percent of households included a married man and woman. Sixty years later, much had changed, and married couples represented only about 48 percent of US households. Birth control is one reason. In the mid-twentieth century, before reliable birth control was widely available, sex often led to pregnancy, and pregnancy outside of marriage was considered shameful. So couples got married partly to enjoy sex without the shame. Divorce was also considered dishonorable in the mid-twentieth century, but that's no longer true. One out of every two modern marriages ends in divorce. And society is much more accepting of same-sex and heterosexual couples making their lives together without marriage.

In the twenty-first century, those who do choose to marry often put a new twist on it. For example, Lisa Haisha and her husband live in separate houses, four blocks apart, in Hollywood, California. She keeps her house super tidy. His is cluttered. She entertains a lot. He likes time alone. Most nights, they have family dinner with their daughter and hang out together until her bedtime. After that, the spouses kiss good night and head to their respective houses—married but not cohabitating.

Then there are Americans who aren't married at all. In 1960, 72 percent of Americans over the age of eighteen were married.

This 1950s advertisement shows the traditional US family of that era—a heterosexual couple with kids. It was Mom's job to care for the children, cook meals, and keep the house clean. Dad worked outside the home.

By 2011 that number was down to only 51 percent. Why are fewer Americans marrying? Some people are focusing instead on graduate school and careers. Others say they are working too hard to commit to a marriage. Many have to pay back hefty college loans and can't afford to get married or start a family. Those who do get married tend to do so later in life. In 1950 the typical American man married at the age of twenty-three and the typical woman married at the age of twenty. By 2010 the ages were twenty-eight for men and twenty-six for women.

For those who choose not to marry, being single doesn't mean being alone. Many Americans meet their social needs through networks of family and friends, and lots of unmarried people are in romantic and sexual relationships. Some couples embrace polyamory, an arrangement in which both partners are free to have other sexual relationships. Brooklyn, New York–based attorney Diana Adams has several partners, none of whom are her legal spouse. She says, "We put so much emphasis on a partner being everything—that this person completes you—and when that doesn't happen it creates a lot of pressure." She says the key to making polyamory work is having lots of open communication among all the people involved.

As for having kids, marriage is no longer a requirement for that either. According to the Pew Research Center, in 2013, 34 percent of US children lived in a single-parent household. Women—both lesbians and heterosexuals—are more likely than men to be single parents. Sometimes single women get pregnant with sperm from a male friend or from an anonymous sperm donor. Others adopt children or become single moms after the breakup of a marriage or a relationship. A woman without a husband used to be an outcast. Those days are over. Judging from changing practices around the world, marriage is headed into new territory.

3
FORBIDDEN LOVE

Not long ago, none of these couples would have been allowed to marry:

> Ashton Kutcher and Mila Kunis
> David Bowie and Iman
> Kanye West and Kim Kardashian
> Taye Diggs and Idina Menzel
> Neil Patrick Harris and David Burtka
> Ellen DeGeneres and Portia de Rossi

KEEPING THE FAITH

In Europe during the Middle Ages, Christians were forbidden to share meals with Jews much less marry them. The actors Ashton Kutcher, who is Catholic, and Mila Kunis, who is Jewish, would have been out of luck had they lived then.

The Quran has rules about interfaith marriages. It says that Muslim men can marry Muslim, Christian, or Jewish women but that Muslim women must marry within the faith.

Interfaith and interracial marriages are no longer taboo. The late singer David Bowie and model Iman came from different religious traditions—Christian and Muslim, respectively. They married in 1992.

In some strict religious communities, members still abide by ancient rules and restrictions about interfaith marriages, but around the world, especially in the West, the interpretation of religious texts has become more flexible. Before the 1960s, only about 20 percent of married couples in the United States belonged to different religions. Even members of different Christian branches—such as Catholics and Protestants—rarely married each other. In the twenty-first century, interfaith marriages have risen to about 45 percent of all married US couples. The trend isn't limited to the United States. The model Iman, who is Muslim, was born in Somalia in northeastern Africa and spent most of her childhood in Egypt. She married outside her faith when she tied the knot with British singer David Bowie, who was raised in (but later rejected) the Christian religion.

One of the biggest decisions interfaith couples make is whether to raise their children in one religion or the other. Some couples decide to expose their children to both religious traditions. Others agree to raise the children in a single faith. Still others decide that religious observance isn't for them.

MURDERED FOR LOVE

In 2016 eighteen-year-old Tasleem was a quiet, beautiful girl, according to her neighbors in Lahore, Pakistan. She was the last person they would expect to bring shame on her Muslim family. Tasleem's crime? Falling in love with the wrong person. The relationship blossomed in secret, because Tasleem knew her family would never accept a Christian son-in-law. Her beloved, Jehangir, converted to Islam, hoping that would be enough.

But secrets were hard to keep in the crowded slum where Tasleem lived.

Men who worked at a steel mill with Tasleem's brother Mubeen saw the couple together. They mocked Mubeen and bullied him, telling him that no real man would let his little sister "misbehave" that way. Mubeen seethed and raged. He yelled at his sister for dishonoring the family by dating a Christian man. He threatened her until she swore on the Quran that she would end the relationship.

She didn't. Instead, Tasleem and Jehangir married in secret. Mubeen learned of the marriage and was enraged. At work, the bullying continued. One of Mubeen's coworkers told him, "What's the matter with you? You are not a man. It would be better to kill your sister. It is better than letting her have this relationship."

> Worldwide, honor-based violence leads to about five thousand deaths per year. . . . They occur in traditional cultures that require girls to be obedient above all else.

Seven days after his sister's marriage, Mubeen bought a gun, returned to the home where Tasleem was living, put the muzzle to her head, and shot her. "I had to kill her," he said. "There was no choice."

In 2015, 1,184 people in Pakistan died in "honor killings" such as Tasleem's. Worldwide, honor-based violence leads to about five thousand deaths per year. Some people mistakenly think that honor killings are based on religious teachings. That's untrue. They occur in traditional cultures that require girls to be obedient above all else. Girls like Tasleem who break the rules are said to dishonor their families. Most nations have laws against honor killings. In highly traditional patriarchal societies, however, the authorities don't always prosecute the killers.

Mubeen was arrested and prosecuted. As he awaits trial in a Lahore jail cell, his father is angry—not at his son but at his daughter. "My family is destroyed," he says. "Everything is destroyed only because of this shameful girl." Their male neighbors agree. One says, "I am proud of this man that he has done the right thing, to kill her. We cannot allow anyone to marry outside our religion." The women in the slum are not convinced. One asks, "Why did she have to die? My husband is having an affair and he left me with four kids to support and no one is killing him. Why?"

"UNTIL DEATH OR DISTANCE"

At weddings, couples commonly vow to stay together "until death do us part." The vow says that the couple is making a lifetime commitment to each other. But during the centuries when slavery was legal in the North American colonies and the United States, making that vow wasn't possible for enslaved African Americans. They were the property of their white owners and could be bought, sold, and passed down to the owner's heirs, along with land, livestock, and money. At any time, a slave owner could sell one of the partners in a couple to another slave owner living many miles away, tearing the couple apart and separating parents from children.

US law did not permit marriages between enslaved Americans. But living in bondage did not stop enslaved couples from falling in love and wanting to join their lives together and have children. Many married in secret. Sometimes a sympathetic white preacher would perform a religious ceremony for an enslaved couple. At wedding ceremonies, the preacher sometimes uttered "until death or distance do you part"—since the couple could be separated if one partner or the other was sold. Other times, the partners celebrated their unions privately by "jumping the broom." In this ritual, which comes from Ghana in West Africa, the couple would declare their intent to be joined in marriage, hold hands, and then jump over a broom placed

An African American couple prepares to jump over a broom—a symbol of sweeping away old troubles and starting anew in married life. The wedding tradition comes from West Africa.

on the ground. The broom symbolized sweeping away the past and making a commitment to a new household. Some twenty-first-century African American couples include this tradition in their wedding ceremonies as a nod to the struggles and heritage of their enslaved ancestors.

LOVE KNOWS NO COLOR

Late one night in 1958, police burst into the bedroom of newlyweds Richard Loving—a white man—and his wife, Mildred—a woman of black and American Indian heritage. The couple lived in Central Point, Virginia, where interracial marriage was illegal. A sheriff put the couple in jail for violating Virginia's Racial Integrity Act of 1924. This law prohibited marriage between whites and blacks as well as between whites and American Indians. The law was designed to prevent miscegenation, or the mixing of races through reproduction.

The ratification of the Thirteenth Amendment to the US Constitution in 1865 had officially ended slavery in the United States. But white citizens continued to control and suppress black citizens through laws that enforced segregation, or separation of the races. For example, in some places, laws forbade white female nurses from caring for black men. In other places, laws made it illegal for black men and white men to play billiards together. Separate schools, hotels, railcars, and baseball leagues for blacks and whites are just a few of the hundreds of examples of legal segregation that endured from the late nineteenth century to the 1960s in the United States.

The specific rationale behind antimiscegenation laws went like this: blacks are inferior to whites, and if a mixed-race couple had a child, that child would automatically be inferior. The foundation for this false belief lay in racial prejudice. It was encouraged by a discriminatory science called eugenics. Based on the teachings of eugenics, governments passed laws and approved of medical practices designed to "improve" the human race by encouraging only "superior" individuals to have children. In this worldview, "superior" individuals were generally able-bodied and white. "Inferior" people, such as blacks or those with developmental disabilities, could be forcibly—and legally—sterilized so they could not have children. Many US states practiced eugenics, including the forced sterilization of poor women of color, in the early and mid-twentieth century. Eugenics was the core philosophy behind a movement to create racial purity in Nazi Germany in the 1930s and 1940s. It led to the Holocaust, in which the German government systematically murdered more than six million European Jews and millions of others, including disabled people, homosexuals, and political protesters during World War II.

In North America, miscegenation laws mostly targeted blacks. But in the American West in the late nineteenth and early twentieth centuries, laws also targeted Chinese immigrants, primarily single Chinese men who worked in railroad construction, mining, and farming. Often white communities demonized these men, charging that they were violent, addicted to opium, and out to steal white women.

By law, Chinese men could not marry white women or bring over a Chinese wife. Laws in both the United States and Canada prohibited Chinese men from sending for fiancées or family members from their home country. Canadian writer Thomas MacInnes, a member of the anti-immigrant Canadian Union of Fascists, didn't want to see any growth in the Chinese population of Canada. His goal was to maintain a white majority and white control in the nation. He wrote in 1927, "It may be very right indeed to separate a man by law from his wife and family if he belongs to a race whose increase in the country would be disastrous to those already in occupation of it."

Fast-forward to the late 1950s, when Richard and Mildred Loving were in love and married—and under arrest. (They had married in Washington, DC, where interracial marriage was legal.) A Virginia judge gave the couple a choice: a year in prison or move out of Virginia for twenty-five years. The couple chose to leave Virginia and make a new life in Washington, DC. But Mildred missed her family and the Virginia countryside where she had grown up. "We loved each other and got married," Mildred said later. "We [were] not marrying the state. The law should allow a person to marry anyone he wants."

In 1963 she contacted US attorney general Robert Kennedy, who helped her begin a lawsuit known as *Loving v. Virginia*. At first, the Lovings faced defeat. In a ruling against them, the lead justice for the Virginia Supreme Court wrote, "Almighty God created the races white, black, yellow [Asian] . . . and red [American Indian], and he placed them on separate continents. . . . The fact that he separated the races shows that he did not intend for the races to mix."

In the 1960s, Mildred and Richard Loving successfully fought to end laws that prohibited interracial marriage in the United States.

But the Lovings continued to fight for justice. With the help of the American Civil Liberties Union, they took their case to the Supreme Court of the United States in 1967. The court ruled unanimously in favor of the Lovings. In his opinion, Chief Justice Earl Warren wrote that antimiscegenation laws were "designed to maintain White Supremacy" and were "odious [hateful] to a free people whose institutions are founded upon the doctrine of equality."

This case paved the way for interracial marriages, like the union of musician Kanye West and reality television star Kim Kardashian and the marriage of actors Taye Diggs and Idina Menzel. The last US antimiscegenation law on the books, in Alabama, was removed in 2000. This change was largely symbolic, as Alabama authorities had not enforced the law for many years. All the same, the law's removal did reflect changing attitudes in the United States. According to US census data, 9.5 percent of American marriages were interracial or interethnic in 2010. That number is rising every year.

HERS AND HERS, HIS AND HIS

Historians say that humans have probably always entered into same-sex relationships. They cite examples from ancient Greece, where same-sex relationships were very public. The Greeks considered a love affair between men, typically an older man with a much younger lover, to be the highest form of human relationship. Plutarch (CE 46–119) was an ancient Greek writer. He described the Lelantine War (ca. 700 BCE), in which the Chalcidians triumphed thanks to a brave general named Cleomachus. Prior to a decisive battle, he called his lover, Anton, to him and asked if Anton would watch the battle. Anton said he would, and "after many tender kisses and embraces . . . Cleomachus's love redoubling his courage . . . he [Cleomachus] charged into the thickest of the enemy and put them to the rout."

Playwrights and poets of the time lauded relationships like that between Cleomachus and Anton. They were held up as examples of pure love. Marriage, however, was not the same as love, and the structure of marriage in ancient Greece was strict. Husbands were in charge. Wives were subservient, and their main role was to bear children. Same-sex marriages were out of the question.

Marriage practices were very different in other parts of the world. Anthropologists studying traditional African societies documented socially accepted same-sex relationships, often including marriage, as late as the mid-twentieth century. Among the Nzima of Ghana, adult men could marry each other. Zande warriors in Sudan took "boy-wives" as well as girl brides. Women in polygamous households were often sexually involved with one another. Women could marry each other in more than thirty traditional African societies, including the Kikuyu, the Lovedu, and the Nuer.

American Indian tribes have traditionally embraced fluid definitions of gender and sexuality. In addition to "male" and "female" identities, more than 155 North American tribes recognize a third gender, called a two-spirit person. Some tribes further divide the third gender into "female two-spirit" and "male two-spirit" individuals, resulting in four distinct gender groups.

Among some tribes, male two-spirits and women were responsible for basket weaving and beading. In other tribes, female two-spirits and men were warriors and hunters. In 1885 an anthropologist took a Zuni two-spirit named We'wha from New Mexico to Washington, DC. As part of a larger cultural mission, We'wha met with government leaders, including President Grover Cleveland, and attended high-society parties. The anthropologist introduced We'wha as a princess, and those she met accepted her as a female, although she was biologically male.

INTO THE CLOSET

While some traditional societies accepted same-sex relationships and gender fluidity, many other societies condemned them. The Old Testament of the Bible says that sex between two men is an abomination and punishable by death. During the Middle Ages in Europe, where laws were based on Christian doctrine, punishments for homosexuals included castration (removal of the testicles) for men and burning at the stake. The authorities often singled out women who lived alone or in other ways did not conform to social norms, labeled them witches, and burned them alive. Historians believe that many of these victims were lesbians.

Starting in the fifteenth century, European Christian missionaries (religious teachers) and conquerors condemned transgender people and same-sex relationships when they traveled to the Americas, Africa, and other non-Christian territories. When Spanish explorer Vasco Núñez de Balboa encountered two-spirits in Central America in 1513, he ordered them put to death. His soldiers directed ferocious dogs to attack and kill them.

Into the twentieth century, most Americans—including psychiatrists—viewed homosexuality and transgender identity as a sin or a mental illness. In many parts of the United States, homosexuality was against the law. A person could be legally fired from a job, jailed, or locked up in a psychiatric hospital for being gay. In the worst cases, hateful assailants beat up and murdered gay people. For safety, most gay, lesbian, bisexual, and transgender people were deep in the closet.

Change came slowly. In the United States, gay men and lesbians began to organize. The Mattachine Society for gay men, founded in 1950, and the Daughters of Bilitis for lesbians, started in 1955, were some of the first groups to fight for gay and lesbian civil rights. Following closely on the heels of the US civil rights movement, the women's liberation movement, and the youth counterculture movement of the 1960s, gay and transgender Americans began standing up for their rights. A turning point came in 1969 when customers at the Stonewall Inn, a gay and transgender bar in New York City, fought back against police who had raided the bar. (Police routinely raided gay bars, arresting patrons.) Another important milestone occurred in 1973 when the American Psychiatric Association stopped classifying homosexuality as a mental illness.

As the movement picked up speed, Americans began to ask, why not marriage rights and protections (such as tax breaks, insurance benefits, and the right to raise children together) for same-sex couples too? Some same-sex couples began to marry in private ceremonies, and eventually some US states authorized same-sex domestic partnerships and civil unions. These legal unions were similar to marriage, though the federal government did not honor them. Other states were not required to honor these unions either. While same-sex unions were gaining ground, many Americans were strongly opposed to them. In 1996 the US Congress passed the Defense of Marriage Act (DOMA). This law defined marriage as a union between one man and one woman. Over the next twenty years, Americans vehemently debated same-sex marriage. Some states defied DOMA, passing same-sex marriage into law. Others enacted bans on same-sex marriage, claiming that marriage was intended by God to be between

ALL IS NOT EQUAL

By 2017 twenty-five nations worldwide had legalized same-sex marriage. Almost all of these are Western nations, with developed economies and liberal attitudes about gender, sexuality, and marriage. However, homosexual sex remains illegal in more than seventy-five countries and is punishable by death in ten countries.

Two women exchange marriage vows. A 2015 US Supreme Court decision held that same-sex couples are legally entitled to wed in all fifty states.

one man and one woman. But in 2011, the tide turned when the US attorney general announced that the US government would no longer enforce DOMA.

About four years later, in April 2015, the US Supreme Court heard oral arguments in *Obergefell v. Hodges,* a case that challenged the constitutionality of state bans on same-sex marriage. After decades of fighting for the decriminalization of same-sex relationships and advocating for gay rights, gay Americans and their allies watched this major civil rights issue take center stage. Justice Anthony Kennedy wrote the court's majority opinion, ruling on June 26, 2015, that "the history of marriage is one of both continuity and change." The justices cited the *Loving v. Virginia* case as an example of constitutional protections for "the right of personal choice regarding marriage." The decision held that "the Fourteenth Amendment [which provides for equal protection of the law] requires a state to license a marriage between two people of the same sex and to recognize a marriage between two people of the same sex when their marriage was lawfully licensed and performed out-of-state."

With that ruling, DOMA and state marriage bans were dead. This was good news for Neil Patrick Harris and David Burtka, Ellen DeGeneres and Portia de Rossi, and millions more same-sex couples who chose to marry. Marriage equality was the law of the land. Once again, love was changing everything.

4
WILL YOU MARRY ME?

When Romeo and Juliet fall in love at a masked ball, they know perfectly well that their families, sworn enemies, will never agree to the match. The play, written by William Shakespeare and published in 1597, is set in Verona, Italy, in the fourteenth century. Romeo doesn't bother asking for Juliet's hand. Instead, the young couple ignore all the usual customs of betrothal (engagement). They marry in secret, defying Juliet's father, who has already arranged to marry her to a relative named Paris. Things do not go well.

A PERFECT MATCH

In choosing spouses for their children, parents of earlier centuries wanted to achieve specific goals. A nobleman might want to cement a political alliance. A farmer might want a skilled baker as a daughter-in-law. Making a love match—or even a friendly match—was low on the list of priorities.

If parents couldn't find a suitable match, they might turn to a professional matchmaker for help, a practice that occurred in

In Europe during earlier centuries, young people were supposed to let their fathers choose their spouses. The fictional Romeo and Juliet, from William Shakespeare's play of the same name, defied their families and married in secret. The photo shows Claire Danes and Leonardo DiCaprio playing the couple in a 1996 film version of the play.

many cultures—and still does in Asia, India, and elsewhere. For example, the Jews of eastern Europe, from the Middle Ages to the early twentieth century, used matchmakers to arrange marriages. In the 1964 US musical *Fiddler on the Roof,* which takes place in a Jewish village in Russia at the beginning of the twentieth century, the town matchmaker is tasked with finding husbands for the milkman's daughters.

Chinese parents also employed matchmakers to identify promising mates, a practice that continues in the twenty-first century. Very wealthy Chinese families might hire high-end "love hunters," paying from $50,000 to more than $1 million for their services. Chinese parents who can't afford a matchmaker can turn to marriage markets held in city parks. There, parents hold signs detailing the physical and professional attributes of a young person looking to wed. This type of matchmaking isn't very effective. One mother sat for four years and received only a handful of inquiries. None of them agreed to marry her son.

PICTURE BRIDES

Japanese men working as laborers in North America in the early twentieth century wanted Japanese brides. To find them, they used a fairly new technology: photography. Their parents in Japan discussed possible matches with the parents of Japanese women also living in Japan. Parents exchanged photographs of their sons and daughters. Once the parents agreed on a match, a wedding took place in Japan without the groom even being present. After that, the "picture bride" traveled halfway across the world to meet her new husband in North America.

The picture bride tradition continues in modern times. The Internet offers access to hundreds of mail-order bride websites, where men can see photos and profiles of women hoping to marry. Many of the sites match American men with women from overseas. (Less common are sites offering mail-order grooms.) In many ways, Match.com and other dating websites are similar— except the partners initially connect with the goal of dating rather than with the express purpose of getting married.

This colorized photograph from the early twentieth century shows Japanese picture brides at a California immigration facility on Angel Island in San Francisco Bay. They have yet to meet their husbands, who are already living in the United States. After exchanging photographs of their sons and daughters, parents in Japan arranged the marriages.

FIVE GOATS AND TEN BARRELS OF WINE

When parents and matchmakers were in charge of arranging marriages, the job didn't end with identification of the perfect match. Instead, the two families began to negotiate financial aspects of the marriage transaction. Marriage was a business deal as well as a social arrangement. Families exchanged gifts and money to cement this relationship.

In most of Europe, from the Middle Ages to the nineteenth century, and in much of Asia, the Middle East, and Africa, from ancient times to the twenty-first century, the bride's family made a payment of money or goods, called a dowry, to the prospective groom or his family. Parents paid dowries to ensure that a daughter began married life with some financial security. The money or goods helped the newlyweds establish a home. Parents sometimes paid the dowry to a new son-in-law in installments. If he didn't treat their daughter well, the husband couldn't collect the rest of the assets.

The amount of money depended on the circumstances of the families involved. Marrying up—into a family with a higher social status—cost more than marrying into a less wealthy family. Since most societies did not value single women, parents needed to find husbands for their daughters. A girl's physical attributes mattered. If she was unattractive, it could be hard to find her a husband, so the parents might offer a larger dowry to sweeten the deal for the groom and his family.

European dowry traditions declined in Europe's North American colonies in the seventeenth century. The majority of the colonists were men who set out alone to make a new life in the New World. They wanted wives with whom to start families and households, but marriageable women were in short supply. Happy to find a wife at all, the men didn't care whether a woman's family had money to pay a dowry, so the dowry system began to fade. The practice of paying dowries continued in Europe until about World War I (1914–1918).

This nineteenth-century watercolor illustration shows an Indian bride bedecked in jewelry. In the Hindu tradition, a bride's jewelry served as her dowry—a gift from her family to the groom.

After that, women began entering the workforce in larger numbers, and dowries were no longer necessary. In the twenty-first century, one throwback to the dowry tradition is the custom of the bride's parents paying for the wedding. (Increasingly, however, families in the United States are splitting the cost of the wedding.)

In other parts of the world, dowry traditions varied by culture. In ancient Hindu marriages, the bride's dowry consisted of elaborate jewelry and other valuables. These assets would give her some financial security if her husband died. In other cultures, the payment went from the groom or the groom's family to the bride's family. The payment was meant to compensate the bride's family for the loss of their daughter's labor. Cash, livestock, property, fabrics, or alcohol could all be part of the required payment, called a bride-price, or tribute. This practice was widespread— from Egypt and Mesopotamia in the ancient world to the Aztecs of Mexico and Incas of South America in the centuries before European conquest.

In the twenty-first century, the dowry tradition continues in parts of the Middle East, South Asia, and central Asia. The bride-price tradition continues in parts of China, Taiwan, Thailand, Turkey, and many countries in Africa. In Somalia, a Muslim nation, marriages include both a dowry and a bride-price. In earlier eras, the groom's family paid a bride-price in camels, but in the twenty-first century, the gift is in cash.

BETROTHED AS BABIES

In twelfth-century Europe, fathers often married off their daughters before the girls reached puberty (reproductive age). They were often married to men who were much older. Men wanted wives who were virgins, and the younger the bride, the more likely she was to be without sexual experience. Pope Alexander III, head of the Catholic Church from 1159 to 1181, didn't think that children should be married. He issued a decree stating that the minimum age for marriage should be twelve for girls and fourteen for boys. Many parents, eager to marry off their daughters to cement family alliances, ignored the ruling.

The Chinese practice of *t'ung yang-hsi,* which lasted into the twentieth century, involved arranging the marriage of a baby girl. The baby was then formally given to her future husband's family, who raised her. At some points in Chinese history, this custom accounted for about 20 percent of marriages. Often the bride and groom were relatively close in age, but sometimes, as in Europe, parents arranged legal marriages between very young girls and much older men. A similar practice occurred in India in earlier centuries, but in that culture, the young bride stayed with her own family until she reached puberty and then she moved in with her husband's family.

Many people in the United States view child marriage as a relic of the past. This is not the case. Between 2000 and 2010, nearly 250,000 American girls under the age of eighteen got married. Some were as young as twelve. Of those girls, 31 percent married men older than twenty-one. The nonprofit group Unchained at Last has documented child marriage in nearly all American cultural and religious groups.

Around the world, thirty-nine thousand girls under the age of eighteen are forced into marriage every single day. That's almost fourteen million girls each year. Many of them are under the age of fifteen. Often their families have arranged for their marriages to much older men. Parents who choose such matches are often poor and can't afford to adequately support or educate their daughters. Pressured by their families and communities, the brides must accept the marriages. The vast majority of these girls live in India. Child marriage is also common in many parts of Southeast Asia and Africa. Teenager Zulie, from Ghana, writes about her younger sister: "I'm telling you my sister's story because it's something that I've been worried about. Her

In this photo from 2014, a man holds a teenage girl in Kenya as she struggles to break free. She has just learned that she is to be married to a man she doesn't know in a distant town. Her family arranged the marriage, and the groom provided a bride-price of twenty goats, three camels, and ten cows.

favorite subject is math. She was 14 years old when a man came to see my father. He offered my father cola nuts and 60 cedis ($40) to marry my sister. My father agreed because he doesn't have the money to send us to school. Now [instead of going to school] my sister just sits and waits for the day she's going to marry."

For child brides, the dangers and the repercussions are serious. Many experience violence and abuse at the hands of their husbands. And early marriage means the end of education and the beginning of decades of childbirth and motherhood. Around the world, every hour, girls between the ages of fifteen and nineteen give birth to about sixteen hundred babies. Pregnancy and childbirth are the leading causes of death for girls in this age range. They die because they live mostly in poor nations, where prenatal care is often nonexistent or inadequate. Birthing facilities are barebones and unsanitary. Many girls are already in poor health—suffering from HIV/AIDS or undernourishment—when they become pregnant. Without education and health care, these teen mothers and their children are trapped in poverty. The likelihood of making a better life is extremely low. The United Nations (UN)—an international humanitarian and peacekeeping organization—considers the forced marriage of girls and women to be a form of slavery. The UN works with global nonprofit organizations to address the poverty and social conventions that lead to forced marriage.

THE SHORT LIST

Arranged marriages, unlike forced child marriages, can be a positive. According to Hindu and Islamic traditions, true marriage is defined as a mutually agreed-upon relationship. In a Muslim wedding ceremony, the cleric (religious official) asks the bride three times whether she is marrying of her own free will. Brides answer yes because they trust that their parents have their best interests at heart and have matched them with an honorable husband.

"NO TOILET, NO BRIDE"

In rural India, a public health campaign launched in 2007 links marriage with improved sanitation. More than 665 million people in India lack indoor toilets or private outhouses. Their only option is to relieve themselves in fields or waterways near their homes. To avoid sexual assault, many women wake up before dawn so they can relieve themselves outdoors under the cover of darkness. Unsanitary conditions like this lead to horrific rates of deadly diarrhea-related diseases. To promote safety and hygiene, the Indian government's No Toilet, No Bride campaign urges parents of brides to insist that potential husbands provide their daughters with a living space that includes a bathroom. The government advertises the campaign with a popular radio jingle: "No loo [toilet]? No 'I do!'" In the first two years of the campaign, Indian families built a total of 1.4 million toilets.

The Indian government has launched several campaigns to provide toilets for all citizens. The No Toilet, No Bride program urges parents not to allow daughters to marry into a household without a toilet. In this photo from 2014, a woman and child stand near a new toilet at their home.

The marriage of Sai Srinivasan and Uma Viswanathan, who are both Hindus from India, is an example of a successful arranged marriage. In seeking a spouse, both wanted matchmaking help from their families. They also wanted to have some say in the matter.

In 1999, when Srinivasan was in his twenties and living in Chicago, Illinois, he asked his family in India to look for a wife for him back home. They placed an ad in an Indian newsletter designed to introduce bachelors to prospective brides. Viswanathan and her family, who were also in India, did something similar. From responses to the ads, both sets of parents then created lists of potential spouses and presented them to their kids. Srinivasan caught Viswanathan's interest. Her brother, who was living in California, flew to Chicago to meet Srinivasan and then arranged a phone call between the couple. Eventually their families in India met in person, and Srinivasan flew to India to meet her. Both agreed to the match. They married in India, and she moved to Chicago with her new husband.

Like this couple, many young people are happy to accept their parents' help in matchmaking. Arshi Mujtaba, a Muslim woman who was born in Pakistan, says of her arranged marriage, "I believe my parents made a good decision for me. If they had left it completely to me, I may not have made a good decision."

ON BENDED KNEE

The gentleman is nervous, or so the story goes. He's agonized over this for weeks. Is this the right time? Is this place romantic enough? Is she the right one? He fumbles with the velvet box in his pocket. He watches her face. What if she says no?

Finally, he gathers his courage and kneels before her, holding out a sparkling ring. "Will you marry me?" This is it—the proposal!

Marriage-by-choice is the norm in most Western countries, and the proposal on bended knee is a classic but relatively new

NO BED OF ROSES

Since 2002 viewers have cozied up to watch love and romance unfold on *The Bachelor*. This ABC reality television show pairs an eligible young man with twenty-five would-be brides. Through a series of group, one-on-one, and two-on-one dates, the bachelor begins eliminating women from the show with the goal of choosing his ideal match. When he is down to two women, the bachelor presents his "final rose" to the woman he likes best.

In twelve of the seasons, the bachelor proposed to the woman with the final rose. Of these couples, only two ended up getting married (one couple has since split) and two others are still engaged. Is reality TV the best way to pick a spouse? Perhaps not, but reality dating does make for good entertainment.

tradition. No one knows for sure where the tradition comes from. Some say it recalls the way a European knight traditionally knelt before his queen in a show of loyalty. Others say it recalls the kneeling position of prayer in some religions. Whatever the origin, the symbolism is clear—honoring the beloved and offering commitment.

Marriage proposals have taken myriad forms over the centuries. In an old English practice, if a young man gave his sweetheart a pair of gloves and if she wore them to church the next Sunday, they were engaged. In a Welsh tradition, a suitor presented a carved wooden spoon to the woman he wanted to marry. If she wore it on a ribbon around her neck, her answer was yes. In most cultures, the man proposes to the woman, but not always. A European folk custom encourages women to propose to men on February 29, or leap day, which comes once every four years. In developed nations, sometimes women propose to their male partner on whatever day they want. And when it comes to same-sex marriage proposals, either partner can pop the question.

DIAMONDS ARE FOREVER

Engagement rings—often made of iron, silver, or gold—have been around since Roman times. In the eighteenth and nineteen centuries in North America, men sometimes proposed by giving a sweetheart a metal thimble. After the wedding, the bride had the cup of the thimble cut off, and she wore the remaining section as a wedding ring. Diamonds weren't attached to engagement rings until the nineteenth century. The gems were so rare and expensive that only royalty could own them.

Traditions changed in 1867, when Boer (Dutch) teenager Erasmus Jacobs discovered diamonds along the Orange River on his father's farm in central South Africa. With this find, the British colonizers of South Africa launched a productive and lucrative diamond industry. Suddenly diamonds were flooding the market. With a plentiful supply, diamonds became inexpensive and average people could afford to buy them. The British owners of several different South African mines joined in a cartel, or business alliance, named De Beers Consolidated Mines. By controlling the diamond market and creating the false idea that diamonds were rare, De Beers could raise prices for greater profits. De Beers also set out to convince people around the world to buy diamonds.

In 1938 De Beers hired the New York–based ad agency N. W. Ayer to write articles about celebrities and their diamonds. An agency strategy document read, "We spread the word of diamonds worn by stars of screen and stage, by wives and daughters of political leaders, by any woman who can make the grocer's wife and the mechanic's sweetheart say 'I wish I had what she has.'"

The agency sent lecturers to US high schools to promote diamond engagement rings as symbols of undying love and commitment. It also launched a print ad campaign with the slogan "A Diamond Is Forever." The effort worked like a charm. In 1940 only 10 percent of brides in the United States received diamond engagement rings. By 1990 the figure had jumped to 80 percent. (The number of Americans getting married

With its mid-twentieth-century "A Diamond Is Forever" campaign, the De Beers company successfully convinced US couples that a diamond engagement ring was a must.

The miracle of love

A girl's joy, flowering like a rose, is radiant and full in the lovely miracle of love awakening. And for her a star, blazing bright as her dreams, will mark this moment always. Her engagement diamond, fair spark of eternity, reflects the light of her happiness in changeless splendor, and treasures its tender message of love until the end of time.

Remember, color, cutting and clarity, as well as carat weight, contribute to a diamond's beauty and value. A trusted jeweler is your best advice. Extended payments can usually be arranged.

a diamond is forever

De Beers Consolidated Mines, Ltd.

has fallen since 1990, and sales of diamond engagement rings have dropped as well.)

In 2016 the global diamond market was worth $80 billion, but the industry has a very ugly underbelly. In many African countries, including Sierra Leone, the Democratic Republic of the Congo, and Angola, warlords and rebels force men and children to work as slave laborers in diamond mines. Proceeds from the diamond sales are then used to arm and pay for brutal civil wars and other violence that have killed almost four million people. This situation was dramatized in the 2006 movie *Blood Diamond*, starring Leonardo DiCaprio and Jennifer Connelly.

Consumer boycotts, government crackdowns, and efforts to verify that workers are not enslaved have reduced the multibillion-dollar trade in blood diamonds (also known as conflict diamonds or war diamonds). However, at least one million miners—both adults and children—still dig by hand under brutal conditions to find the shiny rocks that many American women wear on their fingers.

Proposals can be simple, or they can be elaborate proclamations of love. In Portland, Oregon, Isaac Lamb choreographed a cast of sixty, including a marching band, in his lip-dub proposal to Amy Frankel. While she watched from the back of a car and listened on headphones to "Marry You" by Bruno Mars, the couple's friends and family created an elaborate dance spectacle, which was filmed and posted on YouTube. More than thirty million people have viewed the video. You can search YouTube for "Isaac's Live Lip-Dub Proposal" to see it yourself.

In Georgia, Matt Still went cinematic for his proposal to Ginny Joiner. He enlisted videographer Michael Escobar to make a movie trailer in which Matt asks Ginny's dad for his daughter's hand in marriage. The video depicts Matt racing to a movie theater to find Ginny. Ginny was sitting with her brother in the theater when Matt's trailer came on the big screen. Then real-life Matt ran inside

Some people go to extraordinary heights to propose marriage, sometimes spending thousands of dollars on the proposal.

and proposed to her. She had no idea that she was being filmed the whole time or that the back of the theater was full of family and friends. (Search YouTube for "Greatest Marriage Proposal EVER!!!" to see how it happened.)

Sometimes an outpouring of love can have surprising effects. When Lucas Bane proposed to David Devora in a song-and-dance extravaganza in West Hollywood, California (search Vimeo for "Lucas and David" to see it), he hoped David would say yes—and he did. What Lucas didn't expect was to hear from a former high school classmate who had bullied him for being gay. The man wrote, "If you do remember me, it's probably not positive. . . . I saw your video today on Facebook and wanted to say Congratulations! . . . What you have is awesome." The man went on to apologize for being a jerk in high school. Lucas wrote back, "You've made me feel so validated and hopeful about where the world is headed. You've really given me a gift."

And then there's Greek banker Alexander Loucopoulos. He knew that his girlfriend, Guatemalan architect Graciela Asturias, was fascinated by outer space, so he booked a flight on a modified airplane that lets passengers experience zero gravity, the feeling of weightlessness that humans experience in space. Once they were floating in the plane, he pulled out an engagement ring and proposed. Asturias accepted. You might say the proposal was out of this world!

5
GETTING HITCHED

In the 1987 movie *The Princess Bride,* Buttercup is forced to marry Prince Humperdinck. Dazed by grief after she assumes that Westley, her true love, has been killed by pirates, she weds Humperdinck in a hurried ceremony. Later, when she and Westley are reunited, she confesses that she has been wed to another. He asks if she said "I do."

"If you didn't," he tells her, "you're not married." And that means she and Westley can rekindle their romance!

In the real world, the words, actions, and documents that make two people legally or officially married have varied widely across times and cultures. Among the ancient Hebrews, parents negotiated a written marriage contract, called a ketubah, which specified what assets each spouse brought to the match, the husband's obligations to care for his wife, and how money and property would be distributed if he were to die.

In other societies, no written contract was necessary. All a couple needed to do was express a desire to marry. Two thousand years ago, in the early years of the Roman Catholic Church, for example, couples

In an ancient Jewish wedding tradition, families of the bride and groom sign a marriage contract called a ketubah. This ketubah from Vercelli, Italy, dates to 1776.

officiated at their own weddings. No priest or other authority needed to bless the union or provide a written document. In other ancient cultures, including the Mayans of Central America and the Celts of the British Isles, tying a string or ribbon around the couple's clasped hands, called handfasting, signified the intention of two people to bind their lives together. Prince William and Catherine Middleton included handfasting as part of their wedding ceremony.

But in earlier eras, most parents weren't so keen on having their heirs marry whomever they wanted, whenever they wanted. That was way too much freedom. What the parents wanted gradually became law. In Europe, starting in the thirteenth century, laws prohibited clandestine (secret) marriages and elopements. To be legally married, a couple had to follow the right protocol. After both sets of parents had negotiated the terms of the marriage, the engagement period began with reading of the banns, a public announcement of the upcoming marriage at the local church or town council. Anyone who believed the couple should not marry

In numerous traditional cultures, a couple bound their hands together to indicate their intention to marry. Some twenty-first-century couples have revived the custom, which is called handfasting.

had a chance to speak up. (One remnant of this practice occurs in some modern weddings, when the officiant asks if anyone knows of any reason why the couple should not be married.) As long as no one protested after the reading of the banns, the couple exchanged formal vows in church with witnesses and the official blessing of the priest, parents, and the village.

Historically one primary purpose of marriage was the production of legitimate children, and wedding ceremonies often included rituals to increase fertility. According to a British book of folklore from 1898, fertility would be enhanced if the bride wore "something old, something new, something borrowed, something blue, and a silver sixpence [coin] in her shoe." This custom remains popular in the twenty-first century in the United Kingdom and the United States.

Since procreation was paramount, marriages in Europe in earlier centuries could be invalidated if they were not consummated (completed) through sex. For verification, wedding guests sometimes undressed the couple after the ceremony, placed them in bed, and listened at the door for evidence of sexual activity.

FORCING THE SCARF

Brides didn't always go willingly to the altar. At different times and places in Europe, Asia, Africa, and Central and South America, bride kidnapping was seen as a legitimate form of marriage. Sometimes the "kidnapping" was preplanned by the couple. It was really an elopement, with the woman happy to be carried off by the man she loved. But often the abduction was an act of violence, including rape, carried out by men who couldn't find willing wives. Fathers sometimes objected to the practice. Not because it was brutal and devastating for their daughters but because bride kidnapping was property theft and they lost the opportunity to arrange a beneficial marriage.

Marriage by capture still happens in the twenty-first century. In the central Asian nation of Kyrgyzstan, for example, as many of 40 percent of marriages are *ala kachuu,* which means "grab and run." Sometimes the man and woman are in love and the "kidnapping" is consensual, as in earlier eras. But often men kidnap female acquaintances or even strangers, and the practice has become increasingly violent. Kyrgyz couple Eshen and Tursun, who participated in a consensual "kidnapping" in 1954, explained the change. "We don't like the modern way of bride-kidnapping. When we were young . . . we knew each other well and exchanged love letters before kidnapping [elopement]. Nowadays, young people violently kidnap women and this is not our tradition," said Eshen.

A young Kyrgyz woman named Farida was a victim in 2013. She was a twenty-year-old university student with a boyfriend, when twenty-six-year-old Tyhchtybek kidnapped her. He'd met her only twice, but he thought she was good wife material. With his family's knowledge, he gathered a group of friends, who helped him force her into a car. Back at his house, his family prepared for the forced wedding. After hours of struggling to escape, Farida became too exhausted to resist any longer. Tyhchtybek's female relatives tied a white scarf around Farida's head as a sign of her consent. But Farida's brother had heard that she had been abducted. He went to Tyhchtybek's house to rescue her, saying, "If my sister wants to stay here, I won't stop her. But look at her, she is crying and is saying that she wants to leave. So I will take her back home."

Farida was one of the lucky ones. She was rescued, returned home, and eventually married her boyfriend. Other kidnapping victims aren't welcomed back by their families, however. Once they end up in a kidnapper's home, they are considered to have shamed their parents. They have little choice but to resign themselves to marriage to their abductors. Kyrgyzstan outlawed bride kidnapping in 1994, but the crime is rarely prosecuted there. And bride abduction is not limited to Kyrgyzstan. It takes place in at least seventeen countries, including China, Mexico, Russia, and parts of southern Africa.

MAKING IT LEGAL

If you want to get married in the United States, you must comply with a number of legal requirements, which vary by state. Generally the process starts at the county courthouse. The couple pays a fee and applies for a marriage license. To get the license, the couple must demonstrate that they meet all the necessary conditions:

- They must be of legal age to marry (as young as twelve with parental consent in some states, typically eighteen without).
- They must not be legally married to anyone else.
- They must be entering into the marriage freely.

Many states also prohibit first cousins from marrying, to prevent couples with similar genetic makeups from passing on genetic diseases to their children.

GREEN CARD MARRIAGES

Millions of people around the world, especially in war-torn countries or those with repressive governments, are desperate to live in the United States. But gaining legal admission to live in the United States is difficult and expensive and can take many years. A quicker, easier route to US residency is to marry a US citizen. To do this, some foreign would-be residents enter into sham unions, called green card marriages, with US citizens. (A green card is an identity card that allows a noncitizen to live legally in the United States.) US immigration authorities are on the lookout for such marriages. If they suspect a green card marriage, they might ask questions such as,

> What color is your husband's toothbrush?
> Where did you go on your first date?
> Does your wife like techno music?
> Can you provide pictures of your last vacation together?

If the marriage is a sham, the spouses might not be able to answer the questions or one spouse's answer might not match the other's.

Some US citizens knowingly enter into green card marriages. They agree to marry foreign strangers in exchange for large sums of money—as much as $20,000. Other US citizens are duped. They meet foreigners online or in person, believe they have found true love, and get married, only to find out later that the foreign spouse pretended to be in love to get a green card. The penalties for those who knowingly enter into a green card marriage are high: up to five years in prison and a fine of up to $250,000. For the foreign partner, the penalty includes deportation (return to the person's home country).

Some states impose a waiting period between the application and issuance of a marriage license. Others require waiting between the licensing and the wedding. Others have no waiting periods. An officiant, such as a religious leader, a judge, or another state-authorized official, conducts the ceremony. This person also fills out the marriage certificate, which is signed by the couple, witnesses, and the officiant. The paperwork is then registered with the state, and the couple is legally married.

Anyone who meets state requirements can marry in the United States. For those in a rush to get married, the Little White Wedding Chapel in Las Vegas, Nevada, offers a drive-up wedding window.

The ritual of marriage carries meaning and benefits. Weddings are public announcements that a new family unit is being established. Gifts of household goods and cash can help a couple equip and furnish their home, take a honeymoon, or set up a savings account. From a legal perspective, moving from single to married status provides protections and benefits. A married couple often qualifies for tax credits. One spouse can inherit property and money, tax free, when the other spouse dies. Spouses can visit each other in the hospital and make medical decisions for each other, no questions asked. They can also more easily adopt children.

RED FOR LUCK

Wedding ceremonies are full of symbolism. Rings, dresses, flowers, food, and gifts—almost everything is ripe with meaning. Many of the symbols date back to previous centuries.

The white wedding gown, for example, became popular after Britain's Queen Victoria wore white at her 1840 wedding to Prince

Albert. In Western nations, white is a symbol of virginity. Many twenty-first-century brides wear white wedding gowns, even if they aren't virgins. Japanese brides typically wear white kimonos, often lined with red. Many Ghanaian brides choose brightly colored, patterned fabrics. In China, India, Pakistan, Vietnam, and other parts of Asia, the traditional bridal gown is red to symbolize good luck and a prosperous future.

The wedding outfit for a groom also varies from culture to culture. In the United States and Europe, a black tuxedo or a finely tailored suit is standard. But like Prince William, some Western grooms choose a military dress uniform. Scottish grooms often don kilts—knee-length pleated skirts, traditionally worn by soldiers. In India many grooms wear a sherwani, an elaborately embroidered, fitted jacket that falls to the knee. Among the Yoruba people of Nigeria and Benin in West Africa, a groom might wear a brightly colored, wide-sleeved robe called an agbada over loose trousers.

Ceremonies often include a ritual to mark the couple's transition from their families of origin to their life together. In a Christian or secular wedding in the West, the father (or both parents) often walks the bride down the aisle and gives her away to the groom.

During a Hindu wedding, the bride's mother pours water into the hands of the father of the bride. He then pours the same water into the groom's hands, who pours it into the bride's hands. The transfer of water symbolizes the connection between generations and the continuation of the family heritage.

Many weddings include some kind of exchange. In Western Christian and secular weddings, a couple exchanges wedding rings. In weddings in the Eastern Orthodox Church—the major Christian church of Greece, Russia, eastern Europe, and some parts of Africa and the Middle East—the priest presses the couple's wedding rings against their foreheads three times, and the couple exchanges the rings between them three times. In both Hindu and native Hawaiian weddings, the bride and groom exchange flower garlands. In Gambia and Senegal in Africa, the groom offers kola nuts to the bride's family, and in exchange, they offer him advice about married life.

Water flows from hand to hand in a Hindu wedding ceremony. The bride's hands (decorated with henna) receive the water last. The pouring of water symbolizes the link between families and generations.

A Japanese groom and bride don traditional wedding kimonos.

Japanese couples sip sake (a rice wine) three times from three different cups to show the new family bond. Among the Yoruba, the couple tastes sour, bitter, hot, and sweet foods that symbolize the ups and downs of married life. The sequence ends with sweet foods in hopes of a marriage filled with sweetness. At a Korean wedding, the couple's parents toss dates (symbolizing girls) and chestnuts (symbolizing boys) at the bride. She tries to catch them in her skirt to ensure fertility. At the end of a Jewish wedding ceremony, the groom crushes a wineglass underfoot. Jewish scholars say that the act has many meanings, including an acknowledgment of the fragility of human relationships.

OVER-THE-TOP WEDDINGS

Wedding ceremonies can vary tremendously, depending on faith, culture, and the preferences of the couple. Many twenty-first-century couples merge customs from multiple traditions to create a ceremony that captures their unique personalities.

When April Pignataro told her mother that she and her fiancé, Michael Curry, wanted to get married in a shark tank, her mom was not amused. But April got her way. She donned a white wet suit (the groom wore a black-and-blue wet suit) and scuba gear so that she and Michael could exchange vows underwater at the Atlantis Marine World aquarium in New York. (Search YouTube

TRASH THE DRESS

After the wedding ceremony is over and the official portraits of the couple are taken, some modern brides get a little crazy. The trash-the-dress tradition blends high-fashion photography and nontraditional settings to create unforgettable images of brides in their wedding gowns. But these brides aren't standing sweetly before the camera. Instead, they're climbing trees, getting splattered in mud, floating in the salty ocean, or covering their dresses in paint. These photo sessions, also called "rock the frock" or "fearless bridal" shoots, let the bride be creative and have a little fun after the stress of planning the big day. They also send a defiant message about wedding traditions. The trash-the-dress trend rejects the notion that weddings must be formal and that dresses must be expensive. But some people say that trashing wedding dresses is wasteful. They suggest that brides donate their worn wedding dresses to women who can't afford their own.

for "Wedding with Sharks" to see the ceremony.) The officiant, who was standing outside the tank, communicated with the bride and groom via radio. At one point, he said, "You've expressed your desire to be husband and wife. Can someone move this shark?"

Abigail Kirk and Andy Weeks from Bournemouth, England, got married in a *Twilight*-themed wedding, complete with music from the movie *Breaking Dawn—Part I,* in which the *Twilight* characters Bella and Edward get married. Abigail's wedding dress and the flower arrangements were modeled on those in the movie. These Twihard fans even legally changed their last name to Cullen, which is Edward's last name.

The officiant at Jennifer Landa and Joshua Busch's wedding began with this line: "Love is the force that allows us to face our fear and the uncertainties with courage. Sounds like *Star Wars.*" It sure did! The *Star Wars*–themed wedding included lightsabers, a bridal escort of imperial storm troopers, flower girls with Princess Leia buns, Tauntaun and Wampa cake toppers, and the father of the bride dressed as Darth Vader. (Search Vimeo for "Josh + Jennifer" to watch the wedding.)

Some weddings end up in the record books. According to *Guinness World Records,* the largest wedding ever held took place in Madras, India, in 1995 and included 150,000 guests. A Chinese bride entered the record book with a 1.6-mile (2.6 km) train behind her wedding dress in 2015. And Ohio bride Jill Stapleton asked all 110 students at her dance studio to be bridesmaids at her wedding in 2010, breaking the previous record of ninety bridesmaids.

And then there is money. Vanisha Mittal, the daughter of a billionaire, and investment banker Amit Bhatia spent about $60 million on their 2004 wedding celebration in France. Prince William and Catherine Middleton's spectacular wedding cost about $34 million. And of course, there's reality television star Kim Kardashian. Her 2011 marriage to professional basketball player Kris Humphries lasted only seventy-two days. The price tag?—$11 million!

THE COST OF LOVE

Getting married is big business. From dresses to cakes to flowers and wedding venues, couples can spend a fortune to get hitched (and often feel obligated to do so). In the United States, couples and their families spend about $55 billion a year on weddings. According to a 2016 survey by the Knot, the average wedding in the United States costs $35,329, not including the honeymoon. Here's a budget breakdown for a top-of-the-line wedding:

Expense	Cost ($)
Reception venue	16,107
Engagement ring	6,163
Reception band	4,156
Photographer	2,783
Flowers/decorations	2,534
Wedding planner	2,037
Ceremony site	2,197
Videographer	1,995
Wedding dress	1,564
Rehearsal dinner	1,378
Reception DJ	1,245
Transportation	859
Ceremony musicians	755
Wedding cake	582
Invitations	462
Favors	268
Groom's tuxedo	280
Officiant	278
Total	$45,643 plus $71 per person for catered food

KEEPING IT SIMPLE

For the vast majority of couples, that kind of money is impossible. Georgia's Christina McGinnis and Brian Green wanted to get married, but the planning was stressful, time-consuming, and expensive. "It took away the purpose and excitement of being married," said Green. He planned a surprise flash-mob wedding for McGinnis because, he explained, "the marriage is what's important." McGinnis thought that a close friend needed her to model for a wedding dress photo shoot at the local mall. As McGinnis posed in front of a giant Christmas tree, her father appeared with a bouquet and told her that she was getting married. Suddenly, all her friends and family formed an aisle, her groom and the officiant appeared, and they tied the knot.

Another simple approach is the environmentally friendly wedding. Ideas include holding the ceremony outdoors, in a park or a garden, with only the sun to provide lighting. Printing invitations on recycled paper or sending e-invitations, buying organic flowers, and serving food from local organic farms are other eco-friendly options. Used or hand-me-down wedding outfits are also more Earth-friendly than brand-new ones.

6
CUTTING TIES

A gigantic, gaudy sign outside the Little White Wedding Chapel in Las Vegas, Nevada, advertises a twenty-four-hour drive-up wedding window. The steeple-topped building has hosted more than eight hundred thousand quickie weddings since it opened in 1951. In 2004 twenty-two-year-old pop star Britney Spears and her childhood friend Jason Alexander pulled up in a lime-green limousine for a spur-of-the-moment wedding. Fifty-five hours later, they called it quits. It was not, apparently, a match made in heaven.

AS OLD AS MARRIAGE

Divorce, or the dissolution (breakup) of a marriage, is not a new idea. Written records document divorce in ancient Egypt and Mesopotamia. In ancient Rome, where both marriage and divorce were defined by mutual intent, either spouse could initiate the breakup. In other cultures and eras, only the man got to decide. Among the ancient Hebrews, for example, husbands could divorce their wives, but wives could not initiate divorce. In ancient Greece,

Americans wanting a divorce in the early and mid-twentieth century sometimes traveled to Nevada, which had lenient divorce laws. In this 1945 cartoon, a woman celebrates as she leaves a courthouse in Reno, Nevada, with her divorce decree.

a husband could drop his wife at any time, but if he didn't have a good reason—such as infidelity on her part—he had to return the dowry to her family.

Divorce in the past wasn't rare either. The Ottoman Empire, based in lands that became Turkey, controlled much of the Middle East, parts of North Africa, and parts of southern Europe for more than six hundred years. Ottoman court records reveal that divorce was common there. In North Africa from the sixth to the sixteenth centuries, divorce was a regular part of life among both Muslim and Jewish groups. According to British settlers who arrived in Virginia in the early seventeenth century, the Powhatan Indians permitted couples to divorce if they were not getting along, although the partners were expected to soon remarry and establish a new family unit. In nineteenth-century Japan, one in eight marriages ended in divorce.

"LET NOT MAN PUT ASUNDER"

The one major religion that opposed divorce was Christianity. According to the Book of Mark, Jesus said of marriage, "What therefore God hath joined together, let not man put asunder."

A divorce, whether initiated by husband or wife, was considered contrary to the will of God. In the early years of Christianity, the church didn't strictly enforce the prohibition against divorce. But as Christianity spread across Europe, rules about divorce became increasingly rigid. By the twelfth century, the Roman Catholic Church had declared divorce a no go. A couple could separate if one partner committed adultery or if the man was extremely abusive, but the spouses were not actually divorced. The spouses were allowed to live apart, but neither could remarry. The church could grant an annulment, a proclamation that the marriage had never been valid in the first place. This could happen only if the couple could prove they were closely related, if one of them was already married to someone else, or if the man was impotent and therefore unable to impregnate his wife.

In 1527 the strict anti-divorce laws of the Roman Catholic Church led to a battle between Pope Clement VII and King Henry VIII of England. The king, unhappy and worried that his wife had not produced a male heir, asked the pope to annul his marriage to Catherine of Aragon. Pope Clement refused. The king

England's King Henry VIII was desperate to divorce his wife, but the Roman Catholic Church forbade divorce. So, in 1533, Henry VIII founded a new church—the Church of England—that would allow divorce.

was desperate to marry the younger and prettier Anne Boleyn. He was so desperate, in fact, that he broke with the Roman Catholic Church in 1533 and founded a new church, the Church of England (with himself in charge). The new church conveniently allowed him to divorce his first wife. After Henry got his divorce (and a later divorce from a fourth wife in 1540), the Church of England changed its mind. Until 1857 the church, which remains England's national church, refused to grant divorces.

Like King Henry VIII, many men in the European nobility wanted out of unproductive or unhappy marriages. They used their wealth to make this happen. The church allowed individuals to buy indulgences, or forgiveness from sin, including the sin of divorce. Essentially, buying indulgences was a form of bribery, and only the rich could afford them. In exchange for payment, church authorities would claim to have discovered that husband and wife were related by blood and would immediately offer an annulment. The selling of indulgences and other corrupt church practices led a German priest named Martin Luther to break from the Roman Catholic Church and start a new branch of Christianity—Protestantism—in the early sixteenth century. The Protestant Church allowed divorce in cases of infidelity, impotence, refusal of one of the partners to have sex, or desertion. But the rules were skewed in favor of men. Wives were considered their husband's property, and property didn't just up and leave its owner except in the most extreme cases.

WOMEN BEAR THE BURDEN

In 1827 nineteen-year-old Caroline Sheridan (1808–1877), a witty, beautiful, educated young British woman, married lawyer George Norton. Violence in the marriage began almost immediately, and it escalated. Soon after the honeymoon, they argued. Norton threw an inkstand at his wife. Two months after the wedding, he kicked her in the ribs. The abuse continued through three pregnancies, and all the while, she wrote essays, plays, and poetry. Finally, in 1835, when she was pregnant with their fourth child, he beat her so brutally that she miscarried. Enough was enough. She retreated to her mother's home, without her children and empty-handed.

Under British law, Caroline Norton belonged to her husband, as did her clothes, her jewelry, her children, and the income she earned from her writing. As a husband, he could legally demand sex from her at any time, even if she didn't want it. He could beat her without consequence. He could leave her and if he did, he automatically got custody of the children and all her possessions, such as her clothing and jewelry. In cases of extreme cruelty, a wife could divorce her husband, but she'd still lose everything she owned and lose custody of her children. When British women did divorce, they were often socially shunned and blamed for the failed marriage.

"REMEMBER THE LADIES"

In the 1770s, at a series of meetings, future US president John Adams worked with other colonial American leaders to create laws and guiding documents for the new United States. His wife, Abigail, pleaded with him to include protections for women in the new nation's laws. On March 31, 1776, she wrote to him from their home in Massachusetts, saying, "Remember the Ladies, and be more generous and favourable to them than your ancestors [the leaders of Great Britain]. Do not put such unlimited power into the hands of the Husbands. Remember all Men would be tyrants if they could. If [particular] care and attention is not paid to [women] we are determined to foment a [rebellion], and will not hold ourselves bound by any Laws in which we have no voice, or Representation."

Even if John Adams wanted to "remember the ladies," that's not what happened. The Declaration of Independence says that "all men" are created equal. In fact, as Abigail Adams predicted, it was left to women themselves and their male allies to fight for their rights. That battle is still being fought.

Tying the Knot

Married to an abusive husband, Caroline (Sheridan) Norton campaigned in the 1800s for women's rights in Britain. Her work led to laws that made it easier for women to initiate divorce.

Caroline Norton's efforts to break free from George Norton included publishing detailed descriptions of his abuse. She wrote a public letter to Queen Victoria about the British legal system's unjust treatment of women. At this time, other British women were also fighting for legal rights. Their work persuaded politicians to pass the Matrimonial Causes Act of 1857, which reformed divorce law in the United Kingdom. The law offered women more options to initiate divorce, but it was still one-sided. Under the new law, men could easily dump a cheating spouse. But a woman could divorce an adulterous husband only if he had also committed another offense, such as being abusive or deserting her. (Britain did not eliminate this legal double standard until 1923.)

Despite helping make divorce more accessible to other British women, Caroline Norton never did divorce her husband. Although they separated, she remained legally married to him until his death in 1875.

DIVORCE, AMERICAN STYLE

On the other side of the ocean, divorce laws in the American colonies were more liberal. The specifics varied from place to place. In general, adultery, desertion, and cruelty were all grounds for divorce, which either party could initiate. After the American

Revolution and as the colonies became US states, divorce laws loosened even more. In 1852 Indiana passed a law that allowed judges to grant a divorce for adultery, impotence, abandonment, cruelty, drunkenness, failure of the man to provide for the family, conviction of a crime, and any other reason the judge found proper.

That's not to say that American women had it easy in the nineteenth century. Marriage still, in many ways, favored the husband. In divorce proceedings, women had to show more evidence to prove the grounds for divorce than men did. Sometimes women had to move from their home state to a state like Indiana where it was easier to get a divorce. Even if they could document abuse or adultery, wives were often blamed for their husband's behavior, and as in Britain, women who divorced were stigmatized as failed wives.

Divorce was least common in the southern states. Southern society was generally more conservative than the North. White male landowners ruled the lives of their wives, their children, and the people they enslaved. Divorce was frowned upon, and many states forbade it altogether. South Carolina, for example, did not allow divorce until 1949. Entrenched racism created complex sexual double standards. For example, white landowners routinely raped enslaved black women. The law looked the other way. In the less common situation in which a white woman was found to have a black lover, they both faced abandonment and public shaming. The black man would likely be lynched by a local white mob.

Early in the history of the American women's movement, Elizabeth Cady Stanton argued for a woman's right to divorce. In 1870 she wrote, "I think divorce at the will of the parties is not only right, but that it is a sin against nature, the family, the state for man or woman to live together in the marriage relation in continual antagonism, indifference, disgust." As women gained more rights and freedoms in the twentieth century, divorce laws loosened and society became more accepting of divorce.

CELEBRATING THE SPLIT

A growing trend in divorce is to turn the end of romance and marriage into a party. One professional divorce party planner in Los Angeles charges $5,000 to $20,000 per event, but many people do it on their own for much less. Las Vegas has long been a divorce destination. Since in the mid-twentieth century, it has been much easier to get a divorce in Nevada than in most other states. The divorce party business in that city is booming.

Divorce parties have many of the trappings of weddings—fancy invitations, catered meals, elaborate cakes (*below*), and color-coordinated decor (often in black). Magazines, books, Pinterest, and YouTube are full of ideas for planning and hosting a divorce party. Some former brides have even co-opted the trash-the-dress ritual. They mark the end of a marriage by setting their wedding dresses on fire or cutting them to pieces.

Getting a divorce still wasn't easy. For much of the twentieth century, the law required the parties to go to court and demonstrate grounds for divorce, such as adultery or abuse. Couples had to air their private grievances in front of a judge. That changed in 1969, when California became the first state to allow for no-fault divorce. Over time, other states followed. In a no-fault divorce, the spouses need only assert that their marriage has failed, file legal documents, and legally go their separate ways.

TILL DIVORCE DO US PART

In the United States in the twenty-first century, nearly 50 percent of first marriages end in divorce. And for those who remarry, the statistics don't improve. Two out of three second marriages fail, as do three out of four third marriages. On average, most marriages fall apart within eighteen months. So much for fairy tales. Has love let us down?

Usha Gupta and Pushpa Singh, researchers at the University of Rajasthan in India, measured romantic love over time among Western couples who had married for love and among couples in India who were in arranged marriages. Among the Western couples, scores for love started out very high but dropped over time. The exact opposite pattern occurred with the Indian couples. Their love scores started low. After all, the couples hardly knew each other at first. But over time, the love in their relationships grew and deepened. About 95 percent of marriages in India are arranged, and the divorce rate there is one of the lowest in the world. The United States, on the other hand, has one of the world's highest divorce rates. The takeaway, at least from this study, is that the initial level of passion between two people doesn't hold the key to a long and happy marriage.

Divorce is legal in every country except the Philippines and Vatican City, a tiny city-state that serves as the headquarters for the Roman Catholic Church. Around the world, divorce laws vary from country to country. Divorce laws in the United States vary from state to state.

In a best-case scenario in the United States, divorcing couples split any marital assets—such as real estate, cash, and cars—between the two of them, in a division that seems fair to both parties. They also agree on how to share custody of any children and agree on any child support or alimony payments (payments made by one spouse to help support another). This sometimes happens with the aid of lawyers, sometimes without.

If the couple can't agree, a divorce can drag on for many years and can cost tens of thousands of dollars. Many spouses argue bitterly over the details of a split and take their fight to court. They hire high-priced lawyers (divorce lawyers might charge as much as $650 per hour) to fight on their behalf. Lots of couples go into debt in the course of ending a marriage. On top of that, the newly divided family (if a couple has children) shoulders the costs of maintaining two households instead of one.

In Portugal, couples can divorce by simply filing a request online, but in other countries the process is much harder. To file for a divorce in Nigeria, for instance, you must hire a lawyer. You must gather evidence that your spouse has engaged in an action considered grounds for divorce, such as adultery or criminal behavior. Then you must state your case before a judge. It can take months for the judge to issue a divorce decree. The only other way to get rid of a spouse in Nigeria is to wait until he or she dies.

BROKEN HOMES

According to an old nursery rhyme, "First comes love, then comes marriage, then comes the baby in the baby carriage." And after that? For 1.5 million children in the United States each year, divorce is what comes next. The news that your parents are splitting up is rarely welcome. As one young man wrote when asked about his parents' divorce, "It was tough being 10 years old and not understanding why your dad has to leave and why your mother cries herself to sleep at night."

Is divorce really bad for kids? According to researchers, that depends.

When couples keep their conflicts under wraps, the news of a breakup can be a terrible shock for children. On the other hand, in homes where parents are fighting all the time, separation can be a relief for children. According to researchers, children can rebound after a divorce, but a lot depends on their parents' behavior.

Divorced parents need to find a way to get along. When they disagree frequently, the children suffer. For one young woman, the way her father bad-mouthed her mother was traumatizing. "The hardest part was listening to all the [negative comments] he said about my mom. He still does it to this day."

In earlier generations, experts believed it was always best for children to live in an intact family. Modern researchers say that's simply not true. Studies show that a healthy family environment can take many different forms. Sometimes the family is a single-parent household. Or two divorced parents might share custody, with the kids alternating between two households on a regular schedule. A blended family, where two people who have children from previous marriages join forces, can also be a strong one. What matters most, researchers say, is that children have loving, stable, supportive caregivers.

HAPPILY EVER AFTER

Try binge-watching a bunch of romantic comedies or reading a romance novel and you'll notice one thing pretty quickly: most of the action leads up to tying the knot. Couples put a lot of time, thought, and money into orchestrating epic proposals and throwing unforgettable wedding bashes. But after the bouquets wilt and the cake is devoured, one thing remains—the marriage.

What happens then? In an age when marriages seem to be crumbling left and right, how do you make it work? Is it possible to live happily ever after?

ERIC MARCOUX AND EUGENE WOODWORTH

The day they met, neither Eric Marcoux nor Eugene Woodworth expected to fall in love. Marcoux was in the midst of big life changes, leaving the Trappist monastery (a religious community) where he had been a monk as a young man. Woodworth was a professional ballet dancer, performing with several companies.

It was 1953 in Chicago, Illinois, not an easy time or place to be gay. Woodworth was having lunch with a friend when Marcoux, who also knew Woodworth's friend, chanced into the same restaurant. Both men felt an instant and intense connection.

Woodworth said, "My body went cold. I was feeling electric shock. I couldn't move." Marcoux described an almost physical force that pushed him to approach the table and blurt, "Won't you introduce me to your friend?"

"There was nothing else for me to do," Woodworth added, "other than spend my life with him. From that very instant that we met. That was it."

Long before marriage equality became the law of the land in the United States, Marcoux and Woodworth were married in a nonlegal ceremony by a sympathetic Catholic priest. They celebrated their fortieth anniversary in 1993 with a nonlegal Buddhist religious ceremony. In 2013, after sixty years together, they were legally married in Washington State.

The couple said that the key to their long history together was being willing to be vulnerable. Marcoux added that deep honesty in relationships is "incredible and liberating."

NATU AND KUSUM PATEL

Natu and Kusum Patel had only ten minutes to size each other up. It was 1963 in Anand City, India. Their parents had arranged their marriage and set up a question-and-answer session so they could get acquainted. While their families looked on, the couple talked about his studies and her interests. Mostly, they looked at each other, trying to figure out if this match could work.

A month and a half later, they were married.

The couple have different temperaments. She is chatty and excitable. She loves to visit with friends and travel. He is a quiet, frugal man who loves to read and work in the garden.

FROM ATTRACTION TO RELATIONSHIP: SOME GUIDELINES FOR LOVE

It is absolutely, 100 percent okay not to date or be sexual if you don't want to. Engaging in romantic and sexual intimacy is a big decision, and no one except you gets to decide when you're ready.

If you do decide to start dating, it's important to choose someone who makes you feel safe. A good partner makes time for you, listens when you talk, and cares about making you feel comfortable. A good partner doesn't ignore you, make fun of you, or pressure you to do things you're not ready for. Quality romantic relationships have a lot in common with friendships. They are based on common interests, mutual respect, and genuine support. You should enjoy being with your sweetheart and should take time to really get to know each other. If you feel physically unsafe or are being pressured into sex or marriage, reach out to a trusted friend or adult. You might need their support to get out of an unhealthy relationship.

If you're in a relationship that starts to get more serious and physical, make sure that you plan ahead. You can get information on safer sex practices as well as ways to prevent pregnancy and sexually transmitted infections from online sources such as Scarleteen, a school health clinic, or your doctor. If you find yourself thinking about marriage, don't be in too much of a hurry. Most research shows that the longer you wait to get married and the longer you know your partner before getting married, the more likely it is that your marriage will thrive and last for a long, long time.

How did they bridge these differences? How did they cope when faced with the stress and separation of immigrating to the United States in 1975? Natu Patel said, "Life is an adjustment," and the key is to "develop understanding."

After more than fifty years together, the Patels still do things differently. He likes to stick close to home. She takes trips to

Hawaii and Alaska with their grown children. Neither has regrets about their arranged marriage. They don't always agree, but they never consider separating. When their differences lead to conflict, the couple talks through it. She says, "Conversation is good to unite the family."

About their long marriage, he says, "Happy. Very happy!"

She laughs and agrees, "I am happy!"

EDNA AND ALLAN NICKELL

For Edna and Allan Nickell, it was all about dancing. They met as teenagers in Vancouver, Washington, and Allan taught sparkly, fun-loving Edna to dance. They waltzed and tangoed through their courtship, meeting every two weeks at local nightspots and waiting until they were old enough for their parents to give them permission to marry.

Finally, in 1940, they became husband and wife.

Edna was seventeen, and Allan was twenty.

He drove logging trucks and worked in construction. She worked at a neighborhood grocery store. They also raised a daughter. Through it all, they danced. From ballroom dancing to square dancing, the couple was always cutting a rug—all the way into their nineties.

In 2014 the Nickells were crowned prom queen and king at their retirement home, an honor that sent them into peals of laughter. "That was probably because we danced so much!" she joked.

She offered two secrets to their long and happy marriage: humor and communication.

"Don't be in such a big hurry to call it off," she said. "The young people give up too quick."

He said, "We generally talk things out."

"We have our differences, I guess," she said. "But it seems like we work 'em out. It's hard to explain, you know, because you just do it. A lot of love, that's what it takes."

LOVE IS HERE TO STAY

In the past, saving a family business or keeping peace between neighboring rivals was a powerful incentive to make marriage work. Modern marriage is very different. What does it take to weather the ups and downs of life as a couple?

Relationship experts say that couples who discuss the big issues before they get married have a much better chance of staying together. They need to talk about finances, including how they will invest and spend their money. They need to talk about whether they want children, and if they do, how they want to raise them, especially with respect to religion. They need to talk about how they will resolve arguments, including jealous moments and conflicts with extended family members. They should talk about sex and fidelity too so that each person understands the other's expectations. They need to reveal themselves fully.

A happy couple cuts the cake. Successful, long-term marriages require commitment, communication, and love.

BUILDING CONNECTIONS THAT LAST

Where does love come from? How does it grow? How can we make it last through a marriage that could span more than fifty years? Finding ways to stay connected is important. Psychologist Robert Epstein at the American Institute for Behavioral Research and Technology suggests that couples practice what he calls love building exercises to build nonsexual intimacy. Here are some examples:

- Get in a comfortable snuggling position, and try to synchronize your breathing—to breath in and out at the same time—for two minutes.
- Sit close together, facing each other. Gaze deeply into each other's eyes for two minutes, trying to stay focused on each other.
- Stand about 4 feet (1.2 m) apart. Every ten seconds, take a step forward until you are embracing.

Another key to successful relationships is communication. This includes being able to talk in an open and honest way with your partner as well as being an active listener. Here are some ways you can build connections:

- Practice uninterrupted listening. Let your partner talk for two minutes while you listen and then switch roles.
- Be willing to take on the tough topics. Share your hopes and dreams as well as the things that scare you.
- Make time for face-to-face conversations. Social media can be great, but relationships need time in real life to flourish.
- Take turns planning outings. Finding activities you both enjoy is great for relationships.

For Eric Marcoux and Eugene Woodworth, Natu and Kusum Patel, and Allan and Edna Nickell, the secrets to happy and lasting marriages were pretty simple—communication and understanding, humor and commitment. And love.

But as we can see from the history of marriage, love alone is not enough. Couples must work hard to make it over the long haul. Divorce is easy to obtain in many countries, and unlike in the past, it's not always necessary to be married to build a family. In the modern world, couples often stay together because they want to and not because tradition or family expectations force them to stay together.

Modern families are multifaceted. They include stay-at-home dads, working moms, blended families, interfaith couples, interracial couples, same-sex partners, and families that are charting their own paths in new ways. No matter the shape of any particular marriage, couples join their lives with an eye to forever—companions until the end.

SOURCE NOTES

5 Elizabeth Abbott, *A History of Marriage* (New York: Seven Stories, 2010), 51.

15 Stephanie Coontz, *Marriage, a History* (New York: Viking, 2005), 55.

15 Retha Warnicke, *The Marrying of Anne of Cleves: Royal Protocol in Early Modern England* (Cambridge: Cambridge University Press, 2000), 3–4.

19 Coontz, *Marriage, a History,* 76.

19 Ibid.

20 Ibid, 108.

20 Ibid. 139.

20 Ibid.

22 Sara Mendelson and Patricia Crawford, *Women in Early Modern England, 1550–1720* (New York: Oxford University Press, 1998), 444.

35 Roc Morin, "Up for Polyamory? Creating Alternatives to Marriage," *Atlantic,* February 19, 2014, http:// www.theatlantic.com/health/archive /2014/02/up-for-polyamory-creating -alternatives-to-marriage/283920/.

38 Kathy Gannon, "'I Had To': Inside the Mind of an 'Honor' Killer in Pakistan," Associated Press, October 3, 2016, http://bigstory.ap.org/article /0ddcb44fe2b9416381e44ad35c07314b /i-had-inside-mind-honor-killer -pakistan.

38 Ibid.

38 Ibid.

38 Ibid.

38 Ibid.

41 Thomas MacInnes, *Oriental Occupation of British Columbia* (Vancouver, BC: Sun, 1927), 12–13.

42 Abbott, *A History of Marriage*, 330.

43 Ibid., 331.

43 Ibid.

43 Ibid.

43 Plutarch, "Amatorius," Perseus Digital Library, accessed April 1, 2017, http://data.perseus.org /citations/urn:cts:greekLit:tlg0007 .tlg113.perseus-eng1:17.

47 "Obergefell et al. v. Hodges," Supreme Court of the United States, October 2014, http://www .supremecourt.gov/opinions/14pdf /14-556_3204.pdf.

47 Ibid.

47–48 "Obergefell v. Hodges," *SCOTUSblog*, accessed April 1, 2017, http://www.scotusblog.com/case-files /cases/obergefell-v-hodges/.

55–56 "Two Sisters, Two Different Paths: Early Marriage in Ghana," Girls Not Brides, June 13, 2014, http://www .girlsnotbrides.org/girls-voices/two -sisters-two-different-paths-early -marriage-ghana.

57 Emily Wax, "In India, More Women Demand Toilets before Marriage," *Washington Post*, October 12, 2009, http://www.washingtonpost.com /wp-dyn/content/article/2009/10/11 /AR2009101101934_2.html.

58 Lisa Black, "Arranged—Not Forced—Marriages a Good Match in Many Cultures," *Chicago Tribune*, July 27, 2001, http://articles .chicagotribune.com/2011-07-27 /news/ct-x-0727-arranged-marriages -20110727_1_marriages-family -traditions-stephanie-coontz.

60 Uri Friedman, "How an Ad Campaign Invented the Diamond Engagement Ring," *Atlantic*, February 13, 2015, http://www .theatlantic.com/international /archive/2015/02/how-an-ad -campaign-invented-the-diamond -engagement-ring/385376/.

63 James Nichols, "High School Bully Apologizes to Gay Former Classmate after Marriage Proposal Goes Viral," *Huffington Post*, February 4, 2014, http://www.huffingtonpost.com/2014/02/04/bully-gay-wedding-apology-_n_4724854.html.

63 Ibid.

64 *The Princess Bride*, DVD (Los Angeles: Twenty-First Century Fox, 1987).

66 Joseph Jacobs et al. *Folklore* (London: Folklore Society of Great Britain, 1898), 128.

67 Noriko Hayashi/Panos, "Grab and Run: Kyrgyzstan's Bride Kidnappings," *Newsweek*, November 4, 2013, http://www.newsweek.com/grab-and-run-1634.

68 Ibid.

75 "Wedding with Sharks," YouTube, 1:40, posted by the *New York Post*, June 7, 2010, https://youtu.be/YB8cP430fHo.

75 "Josh + Jennifer," Vimeo, 8:10, posted by Jack Costello, accessed April 1, 2017, https://vimeo.com/112105182.

77 "Flash Mob Surprise Wedding at Mall," YouTube, 3:54, posted by "Smingde," December 26, 2014, https://www.youtube.com/watch?v=1poCnUuIgR8.

77 Ibid.

79 Mark 10:9 (King James Version).

82 L. H. Butterfield, ed., *Adams Family Correspondence*, vol. 1 (Cambridge, MA: Belknap Press of Harvard, 1963), 370.

84 Ann Gordon, ed. *The Selected Papers of Elizabeth Cady Stanton and Susan B. Anthony: Against an Aristocracy of Sex, 1866 to 1873* (New Brunswick, NJ: Rutgers University Press, 2000), 342.

87 Brittney Wong, "Seven Ways Divorce Affects Kids, According to the Kids Themselves," *Huffington Post,* August 28, 2014, http://www.huffingtonpost.com/2014/08/28/kids-and-divorce-_n_5730980.html.

88 Ibid.

90 Jennifer Willis, "For 60 Years, 'There Wasn't Anything Else,'" *Portland Oregonian*, January 3, 2013, http://www.oregonlive.com/living/index.ssf/2013/01/northwest_love_stories_for_60.html.

90 Ibid.

90 Ibid.

90 Ibid.

91 Jennifer Willis, "'Different Nature' Nurtured," *Portland Oregonian*, August 1, 2013, http://www.oregonlive.com/living/index.ssf/2013/08/northwest_love_stories_differe.html.

92 Ibid.

92 Ibid.

92 Ibid.

92 Jennifer Willis, "Northwest Love Stories: Edna and Allan Nickell Share 73 Years of Love and a Full Dance Card," *Portland Oregonian*, last modified June 3, 2014, http://www.oregonlive.com/living/index.ssf/2014/01/nw_love_story_edna_and_allan_n.html.

92 Ibid.

92 Ibid.

92 Ibid.

GLOSSARY

adultery: sexual relations with someone other than one's spouse. In some ancient societies, adultery was considered a crime. Many modern cultures consider it to be grounds for divorce.

annulment: a declaration stating that a marriage is invalid. Religious groups and governments can annul marriages for various reasons. For example, if spouses are found to be close relatives, their marriage might be annulled.

betrothal: a promise that two people will be married

bride-price: a payment made by the groom's family to the bride's family. Traditionally, the bride-price was made to compensate a father for the loss of his daughter's labor.

divorce: the act of legally dissolving a marriage

double standard: a set of rules that applies differently or more strictly to one group than to another. For example, society frequently condemns women, but not men for sexual promiscuity.

dowry: property, money, or goods that a bride's family gives to a groom or to his family at the start of a marriage. A dowry helps ensure that a bride begins married life with some financial security. Dowry traditions vary by culture.

engagement: a promise or contract for a future marriage

eugenics: an attempt to improve human society by encouraging certain people to have children and by preventing other people from having children. Twentieth-century US miscegenation laws, which made it a crime for a black person to marry a white person, were based on eugenics. They reflected the erroneous idea that blacks are inferior to whites and that a mixed-race couple would have "inferior" children.

gender: the behavioral, cultural, and psychological norms, feelings, and practices that identify a person as masculine or feminine. Gender is distinct from a person's biological sex, which is determined by reproductive body parts.

heterosexual: a person who feels sexual desire toward those of the opposite sex

homosexual: a person who feels sexual desire toward those of the same sex

honor killing: the murder of a family member who is thought to have disgraced or shamed the family. In some cultures, a girl or woman who has premarital sex or who weds someone of a different religion might be killed for dishonoring the family. Typically, male relatives carry out honor killings.

illegitimate child: an offspring born to parents who are not married to one another. In earlier eras in many cultures, illegitimate children had no legal standing within a family and could not inherit wealth, title, or property. US law no longer makes a distinction between legitimate and illegitimate children.

impotence: the inability of a man to engage in sexual intercourse with and thereby impregnate a woman. In earlier eras in many cultures, impotence was considered grounds for divorce.

infertile: when a woman is incapable of becoming pregnant or a man is incapable of impregnating a woman

legitimate child: an offspring born to a married couple. In earlier eras and in many cultures, only legitimate children had full legal standing within a family. They could inherit wealth, title, and property.

levirate marriage: the forced marriage of a widow to the brother of her dead husband. Common in some ancient cultures, the marriage prevented the widow from marrying a new husband who was not related by blood to the old one. The goal of levirate marriages was to keep wealth within the same family.

LGBTQ+: an abbreviation for lesbian, gay, bisexual, transgender, queer/questioning, and others

marriage equality: the right to legal marriage for same-sex couples, including all legal benefits and protections provided to married heterosexual couples

miscegenation: marriage or sexual relations between people of different races. In the twentieth century, many US states prohibited miscegenation, especially between a white person and an African American person.

monogamy: being in a marriage or a sexual relationship with only one person at a time. Monogamy is the norm in Western cultures in the twenty-first century.

plural marriage: a general term for marriage to more than one person at a time

polyamory: a lifestyle that allows for open sexual and intimate relationships with more than one partner at a time

polyandry: marriage of a woman to more than one husband at one time

polygamy: a general term for marriage to more than one person at a time

polygyny: marriage of a man to more than one wife at a time. Many ancient societies allowed a man to have more than one wife, and the practice continues in the twenty-first century in some parts of the world.

transgender: having a sense of gender identity that does not correspond to a person's anatomy or to the sexual designation a person was given at birth

SELECTED BIBLIOGRAPHY

Abbott, Elizabeth. *A History of Marriage.* New York: Seven Stories, 2010.

Black, Lisa. "Arranged—Not Forced—Marriages a Good Match in Many Cultures." *Chicago Tribune,* July 27, 2001. http://www.humbleisd.net/cms/lib2/TX01001414 /Centricity/Domain/2311/Arranged.docx.

Coontz, Stephanie. *Marriage: A History.* New York: Viking, 2005.

Epstein, Robert. "How Science Can Help You Fall (and Stay) in Love." *Scientific American,* January/February 2010. https://www.scientificamerican.com/article /look-of-love/.

Foreman, Amanda. "The Heartbreaking History of Divorce." *Smithsonian,* February 2014. http://www.smithsonianmag.com/history/heartbreaking-history-of-divorce -180949439/.

Friedman, Uri. "How an Ad Campaign Invented the Diamond Engagement Ring." *Atlantic,* February 13, 2015. http://www.theatlantic.com/international/archive /2015/02/how-an-ad-campaign-invented-the-diamond-engagement-ring/385376/.

Gannon, Kathy. "'I Had To:' Inside the Mind of an 'Honor' Killer in Pakistan." Associated Press, October 3, 2016. http://bigstory.ap.org/article/0ddcb44fe2b941 6381e44ad35c07314b/i-had-inside-mind-honor-killer-pakistan.

Graff, E. J. *What Is Marriage For?* Boston: Beacon, 1999.

Hayashi/Panos, Noriko. "Grab and Run: Kyrgyzstan's Bride Kidnappings." *Newsweek,* November 4, 2013. http://www.newsweek.com/grab-and-run-1634.

Leyser, Henrietta. *Medieval Women: A Social History of Women in England, 450–1500.* New York: St. Martin's, 1995.

Mendelson, Sara, and Patricia Crawford, *Women in Early Modern England, 1550– 1720.* New York: Oxford University Press, 1998.

Morin, Roc. "Up for Polyamory? Creating Alternatives to Marriage." *Atlantic,* February 19, 2014. http://www.theatlantic.com/health/archive/2014/02/up-for -polyamory-creating-alternatives-to-marriage/283920/.

Nichols, James. "High School Bully Apologizes to Gay Former Classmate after Marriage Proposal Goes Viral." *Huffington Post,* February 4, 2014. http://www .huffingtonpost.com/2014/02/04/bully-gay-wedding-apology-_n_4724854.html.

Wax, Emily. "In India, More Women Demand Toilets before Marriage." *Washington Post,* October 12, 2009. http://www.washingtonpost.com/wp-dyn/content/article /2009/10/11/AR2009101101934_2.html.

Wong, Brittney. "7 Ways Divorce Affects Kids, according to the Kids Themselves." *Huffington Post,* August 28, 2014. http://www.huffingtonpost.com/2014/08/28 /kids-and-divorce-_n_5730980.html.

FURTHER INFORMATION

Books

Ali, Nujood, and Delphine Minoui. *I Am Nujood, Age 10 and Divorced*. New York: Crown, 2010.

Andryszewski, Tricia. *Same-Sex Marriage: Granting Equal Rights or Damaging the Status of Marriage?* Minneapolis: Twenty-First Century Books, 2012.

Ansari, Aziz, and Eric Klinenberg. *Modern Romance*. New York: Penguin Books, 2016.

Behnke, Alison Marie. *Up for Sale: Human Trafficking and Modern Slavery*. Minneapolis: Twenty-First Century Books, 2015.

Cenziper, Debbie. *Love Wins: The Lovers and Lawyers Who Fought the Landmark Case for Marriage Equality*. New York: William Morrow, 2016.

Ehrman, Edwina. *The Wedding Dress: 300 Years of Bridal Fashions*. London: V&A, 2014.

Gay, Kathlyn. *Divorce: The Ultimate Teen Guide*. Lanham, MD: Rowman & Littlefield, 2014.

Higgins, Nadia Abushanab. *Feminism: Reinventing the F-Word*. Minneapolis: Twenty-First Century Books, 2016.

Idzikowski, Lisa. *Honor Killings*. New York: Greenhaven, 2017.

Risman, Barbara J., and Virginia Rutter. *Families as They Really Are*. 2nd ed. New York: W. W. Norton, 2015.

Sickels, Carter, ed. *Untangling the Knot: Queer Voices on Marriage, Relationships and Identity*. Portland, OR: Ooligan, 2015.

Squire, Susan. *I Don't: A Contrarian History of Marriage*. New York: Bloomsbury, 2008.

Wittenstein, Vicki Oransky. *Reproductive Rights: Who Decides?* Minneapolis: Twenty-First Century Books, 2016.

Worden, Minky. *The Unfinished Revolution: Voices from the Global Fight for Women's Rights*. New York: Seven Stories, 2012.

Websites

The Feminist Bride
> http://thefeministbride.com/
> The Feminist Bride calls itself "A Wedding Site Inspiring Couples to Walk Down the Aisle as Equals." The site includes information about the history of marriage, alternatives to traditional weddings, marriage equality, global women's rights, and much more.

Girls Not Brides
> http://www.girlsnotbrides.org/about-child-marriage/
> Girls Not Brides is an international organization committed to ending child marriage so that girls can finish their education and choose their own paths in life. The organization's website includes statistics and stories about child marriage and information on efforts to end the practice.

Honour Based Violence Resource Center
http://hbv-awareness.com/
Hosted by the Honour Based Violence Awareness Network, this website offers sobering statistics about honor killings, along with articles and links to more information.

Marriage Equality USA
http://www.marriageequality.org/
Marriage equality became a reality in the United States in 2015, but LGBTQ+ Americans still face discrimination, harassment, and threats to their rights and freedoms. Marriage Equality USA provides information on same-sex marriage and LGBTQ+ rights in the United States and around the world.

Reno Divorce History
http://renodivorcehistory.org
In the twentieth century, Reno, Nevada, was called the Divorce Capital of the World. This website includes fascinating photos, interviews, and historic materials about the city's divorce industry.

Films

Case against 8. DVD. New York: HBO Documentary Films, 2014.
This documentary film examines the fight to overturn California's ban on same-sex marriage, a fight that ultimately went to the US Supreme Court.

Divorce Corp. DVD. Jackson, WY: Candor Entertainment, 2014.
This documentary exposes the ways in which the $50 billion a year divorce industry exploits and often bankrupts struggling families.

The Loving Story. DVD. Brooklyn, NY: Icarus Films, 2011.
This documentary tells of the struggle of Mildred and Richard Loving, an interracial couple who successfully fought to strike down antimiscegenation laws in the United States. A Hollywood movie about their story, called *Loving*, was nominated for an Academy Award in 2016.

Meet the Patels. DVD. Los Angeles: Four in a Billion Pictures, 2015.
In this lighthearted documentary, an Indian American man decides to look for a wife in the traditional Indian way, with the matchmaking help of his parents and extended family—with often hilarious results.

112 Weddings. DVD. New York: Zeitgeist Films, 2014.
After nearly twenty years of filming weddings, a videographer revisited 112 of the couples to see how their marriages were fairing. This documentary film reveals the stories he uncovered.

INDEX

PHOTO ACKNOWLEDGMENTS

The images in this book are used with the permission of: iStockphoto.com/MKucova (decorative frames); iStockphoto.com/andersboman (orange block); iStockphoto.com/scanrail, p. 1; Suzanne Plunkett - WPA Pool/Getty Images, p. 5; Wellcome Library, London/Wikimedia Commons (CC BY 4.0), p. 7; Graham Prentice/Alamy Stock Photo, p. 10; David Wall/Alamy Stock Photo, p. 12; INTERFOTO/Alamy Stock Photo, p. 15; PRISMA ARCHIVO/Alamy Stock Photo, p. 19; The Granger Collection, New York, p. 23; MIKE HUTCHINGS/AFP/ Getty Images, p. 27; Bettmann Archive/Getty Images, p. 30; John Henshall/Alamy Stock Photo, p. 32; Image courtesy of The Advertising Archives, pp. 34, 61; Kristin Callahan/Everett Collection/Alamy Stock Photo, p. 37; Hill Street Studios/Stockbyte/Getty Images, p. 39; AP Photo, p. 42; Maskot/Getty Images, p. 47; Moviestore collection Ltd/Alamy Stock Photo, p. 50; Courtesy of California State Parks. Image 231-18-66, p. 51; © The Stapleton Collection/ Bridgeman Images, p. 53; REUTERS/Siegfried Modola, p. 55; © HARISH TYAGI/EPA/ Redux, p. 57; iStockphoto.com/mrPliskin, p. 62; Heritage Image Partnership Ltd/Alamy Stock Photo, p. 65; aastock/Shutterstock.com, p. 66; Fraser Hall/Robert Harding/Getty Images, p. 70; Nikhil Gangavane/Alamy Stock Photo, p. 72; Ron Koeberer/Getty Images, p. 73; © Rikki Lim/ Pixoto.com, p. 74; Special Collections, University of Nevada Reno Library, p. 79; Pictorial Press Ltd/Alamy Stock Photo, p. 80; Hulton-Deutsch Collection/CORBIS/Corbis/Getty Images, p. 83; Francisco Martinez/Alamy Stock Photo, p. 85; VStock/Alamy Stock Photo, p. 93.

Front cover: Hill Street Studios/Stockbyte/Getty Images (top left); Syda Productions/ Shutterstock.com (top right); iStockphoto.com/triloks (bottom).

ABOUT THE AUTHOR

Amber J. Keyser is an evolutionary biologist-turned-writer who lives on the dry side of Oregon with her husband, two kids, and a dog that looks like a Muppet. Her recent books include *Pointe, Claw*, a novel about two girls claiming the territory of their own bodies; *Underneath It All: A History of Women's Underwear*; *The V-Word*, an anthology of personal essays by women about first-time sexual experiences; *The Way Back from Broken*, a heart-wrenching novel of loss and survival; and *Sneaker Century: A History of Athletic Shoes*. She is the coauthor with Kiersi Burkhart of the middle grade series Quartz Creek Ranch. Visit her website at www.amberjkeyser.com.